COURAGEOUS
FAITH

COURAGEOUS
FAITH

A LIFELONG
PURSUIT OF
FAITH OVER FEAR

DEBBYE TURNER BELL

Our Daily Bread
Publishing™

Courageous Faith: A Lifelong Pursuit of Faith over Fear
© 2021 by Debbye Turner Bell

Interior design by Sherri L. Hoffman

ISBN: 978-1-64070-022-2

Library of Congress Cataloging-in-Publication Data

Names: Turner Bell, Debrah Lynn, 1965-, author.
Title: Courageous faith : a lifelong pursuit of faith over fear /
Debbye Turner Bell.
Description: Grand Rapids, MI : Our Daily Bread Publishing, [2021] |
Summary: "In this book you'll discover faith-filled principles to use as
a blueprint for perseverance, and a new definition of success for your
life"-- Provided by publisher.
Identifiers: LCCN 2021016842 | ISBN 9781640701090
Subjects: LCSH: Success--Religious aspects--
Christianity. | BISAC: RELIGION
/ Christian Living / Inspirational
| SELF-HELP / Personal Growth / Success
Classification: LCC BV4598.3 .T87 2021 | DDC 248.4--dc23
LC record available at https://lccn.loc.gov/2021016842

Printed in the United States of America
21 22 23 24 25 26 27 28 / 8 7 6 5 4 3 2 1

Gussie Lee Turner was a force of nature. I've never met anyone more generous, compassionate, determined, and resilient. Everything I know about God, His Word, and my place in God's Kingdom, I learned from her. Everything I know about being a woman of principle, excellence, and service, I learned from Gussie Turner. By God's grace, I am who I am because of this phenomenal woman. She was known to many as a teacher, preacher, counselor, healer, comforter, advisor, and friend. To me, she was Mommy.

Mommy, this book is for you.

Contents

Prologue

I *don't understand, God! I don't understand! I don't understand.*

In my hotel room after not winning the Miss Arkansas title for the third time, that's all I could choke out through heaving sobs while curled up on the floor in a fetal position—broken, bewildered, devastated. This was the hardest I had ever cried.

After several minutes of sobbing, I finally quieted. I had run out of tears and I was spent, like I had run an ultramarathon. I barely had the strength to breathe.

And I was a mess. Still in my competition evening gown, I no longer had the grace and splendor of a couple of hours earlier. My makeup pooled around my neck. Mascara was a distant memory. And my hair? My "do" was done.

Crying may not change things, but it can open us up to possibilities.

Lying there on the floor of my hotel room like a wrung-out sponge, I could hear my heart beating. And I heard "a voice" speak.

Debbye, I'm faithful. Now get up.

I heard those words clearly in my heart. I know, God speaking to individual people is quite controversial. But for those of us who have heard that still, small voice right as our lives changed—we know it's real. I believe I heard my Creator that night. And those words were manna from heaven. So I picked myself up off the floor, washed my face, took a shower, put on some sweats, and went down to have dinner with my family.

Getting up is hardest when we least expect failure.

I had been so sure I was going to win this time. I had no doubt. All indications pointed to me being the next Miss Arkansas, and our state's representative at the Miss America pageant.

My church had prayed for me. The Bible study group that my mom led in our home every Thursday night had prayed for me. And there had even been "words from the Lord" from various people:

"God said that you are going to win."

"The Lord has given you the victory!"

And I believed them.

Besides, I was not new to this scene. I'd made it to the Miss Arkansas pageant twice before. I knew how to walk across the stage. I knew how to do my turns and poses. I played the marimba, a percussion instrument similar to the xylophone, with abandon. And I was good at the interview portion of the competition.

Plus, I'd placed second at Miss Arkansas the year before. Second place in the pageant world is known as "first runner-up." There was a long-standing tradition at the Miss Arkansas pageant that the previous first runner-up usually returned and won the pageant the next year. That had happened something like five years in a row.

And this year *I* was that person. *I* was the returning first runner-up, for Pete's sake! The press had predicted I would win. I was the crowd favorite.

I know to the casual observer this doesn't seem like a big deal. I mean, it was just a pageant, right? Wrong. For me, it was everything.

I had dedicated my life to pageant competitions the previous six years—a third of my young life. The potential scholarship award could pay for the veterinary education I fervently wanted. I practiced the marimba three hours a day. I read copious numbers of newspapers and news magazines so that I would be knowledgeable about current events and have opinions on social issues. I repeatedly practiced my walking and turning (a big deal in pageant land). I dieted. I exercised. I practiced my public speaking and communication skills. I believed that it was my destiny to become Miss Arkansas. For years I had spent nearly every free moment working toward that goal.

It was my dream. It was my life goal. It was my time.

——————

The results of the competition were being announced. The emcee said, "And the third runner-up is . . ." and I prayed silently, *Lord, your will be done.*

They called someone else's name. *Whew! Thank You, Lord!* Then the emcee bellowed, "And the second runner-up is . . ." and I prayed silently again, *Lord, Your will be done.* They called someone else's name.

Finally, the emcee declared, "The first runner-up is . . ."

God, Your will be done, I prayed as he spoke.

Even though I didn't want to be first runner-up again, I wanted what God wanted. Even if that meant the dastardly first-runner-up placement.

Finally, the emcee finished, "And the first runner-up is . . . (I'm pretty sure there was a drum roll) Debbye Turner."

With those words, my heart broke in a way that it never had before. I couldn't believe my ears. The crowd seemed stunned too. When my name was called, there was an audible gasp from the audience. Most people thought I would win. I had been declared the "odds-on favorite" by the local newspaper. I got huge cheers every time I stepped on the stage that night during competition.

But it wasn't to be.

When I heard God speak to me after that Miss Arkansas pageant, I had a choice to make—one that would affect the rest of my life. It seemed a small choice at the time, but it was monumental. The course of my life hung in the balance. It came down to this: would I quit, or would I continue?

God had told me to get up. He wanted me to keep going.

Getting up after an unexpected loss is the pivotal choice each of us must make nearly every day. Quit or continue? Give up or get up? Lie on the floor of our lives or keep going?

For me, getting up off the floor of that hotel room was the start of learning how to live—not according to my definitions of success but according to God's.

Maybe you're on the "floor" of your life right now. I invite you into my journey of discovery of renewed passion and purpose. Let me share with you some of the life lessons that I have learned, by God's grace.

"How did you do it?"

I heard that question countless times during my reign as Miss America. From hopeful contestants, inquisitive elementary students, sweet grandmas—even from men.

Sometimes the query was incredulous: How did *you* do it?

Everybody wanted to know how this little Black girl from Jonesboro, Arkansas, ended up winning one of the most iconic titles in the world. The Miss America pageant is a US competition, but it is esteemed around the world.

I soon realized, the question wasn't about *process* but *possibility*. People wanted to know how they, too, could achieve a seemingly impossible dream or conquer all odds and realize success, especially after a setback. They wanted to know which areas of life could trip them up and which strategies might give them the winning edge.

People *still* want to know.

This book is, in essence, my answer. In it, I unabashedly share the life principles that led to my success. I open up my life, offering glimpses into some very personal stories that I hope will help you strive for success—no matter what.

People might read some sections of this book and think it's TMI: too much information. But I believe transparency is essential for success. I also know we often fail because we think we are the only ones grappling with certain situations. While getting a long look into my life, hopefully you will discover that you are not alone.

As Miss America, I especially enjoyed speaking with young people. I could be me—just Debbye—the girl who had a dream come true. I encouraged young people to dream big, to work hard, and to never give up. I used my own journey to the Miss America crown as an example of how they could succeed against the odds.

My goal for this book is the same. I want you to dream big, work hard, never give up—and succeed. Succeed in being and doing *all* that God has for you in this life. *Nothing less!*

Many factors play a role in success. Throughout these pages I share ten. At any given time, a combination of them will help you stay on your path. But how they operate in your life will be very different from how they have in mine. And that's OK. My hope is that you are inspired to move from complacency to action, from fear to faith, from failure to success.

ONE

Failure

Everyone fails. The difference between you and someone else is what you do with that failure.

As you read this book, my story, the first thing I want you to realize is that I failed. Many times I didn't win. Often I fell flat on my face. Frequently I was left in a puddle of tears, just like that day when I lost the Miss Arkansas pageant *for the third time*. But out of my failure, I eventually found the power to succeed.

Perhaps you long to turn your hobby into a small business.

Perhaps your deep desire is to win at the Olympics.

Perhaps you want to become an accomplished musician.

Perhaps your goal is to be the best possible parent for your child.

Perhaps you want to turn your empty nest into a bed-and-breakfast.

Perhaps you dream, as I did, of becoming a veterinarian.

Whatever your dream is, know you will fail more times than not. Also know that failure builds the foundation for your success.

Every Olympic gymnast has fallen from the uneven bars. Many times. In fact, it's those falls that she has learned from, that have honed her routines, have trained her to perform at a level of success.

Every musician has played a wrong note. Many wrong notes, in fact. Sometimes an entirely wrong key. But it's those mistakes that shape the musician's skill. Those wrong notes become the basis for the musician to play beautifully, almost perfectly.

Every mom has said the wrong thing to her kids at some time or other. Yet it's those very moments of failure and learning from failure that pave the way for deeper and more loving relationships.

Too often when people encounter failure, they allow themselves to be crushed by it. They let it get them down, allow it to be a negative force in their lives. I have learned to not be afraid to fail. In fact, I have learned to expect some failures. They are the necessary building blocks of breakthrough, triumph, victory.

> Who is depending on you to dream big and succeed?
>
> How does knowing *everyone fails* provide a safety net to pursue success?
>
> By refocusing from *my dream* to *God's will,* how might you view failure differently?

Looking back, it seems obvious to me now that God's hand was at work in my life, but at age sixteen I wasn't particularly concerned about my spiritual purpose and destiny. I was just interested in having some fun.

Elizabeth Howard, the choir director at my church, had always loved young people and looked for positive ways to keep us involved in the community—and out of trouble. She didn't see enough opportunities for young African American girls to develop poise, self-esteem, and confidence, so she started her own local chapter of the national pageant organization Miss Black Teenage World, and recruited girls in our community to participate.

Dynamic and driven, Sister Liz, as she was called, also directed the pageant. It was through this opportunity that I entered the world of pageant competitions.

None of us had been to modeling school, so for several weeks leading up to the pageant, Sister Liz held workshops every Saturday to teach us how to walk on stage and present ourselves with a modicum of grace in all we did. Thanks to her efforts, the friendship and camaraderie of our group of girls transcended the competition and we became close.

Nevertheless, I still wanted to win!

Camille Williams was the brightest star on the night of the big competition and was crowned Jonesboro's Miss Black Teenage World. I placed a respectable first runner-up, technically second place. (This was the first of my long string of first-runner-up finishes.)

I came away from that experience with an important self-discovery: I enjoyed being on stage. I was not afraid of a crowd and I found it invigorating to present myself and receive the audience's acceptance and applause.

Soon after that experience, my high school counselor announced that the America's Junior Miss program was looking for participants. The program was in its prime in those days. Each year, a crop of fresh-faced, sweet-as-pie girls worked their way through the Junior Miss program to make it to the finals, which were televised nationally.

Junior Miss was a teen scholarship organization and careful not to call itself a pageant or a competition. There was no swimsuit competition. No crown. It was a scholastic achievement program designed for teens entering their senior year in high school, and focused primarily on academics, community involvement, character, and personality.

I thought it would be fun to participate, so I signed up. I happened to win the regional title of Northeast Arkansas Junior Miss, which led me to compete at the state level.

To their credit, the organizers were truly interested in developing the minds and spirits of participants. We were discouraged from thinking about winning. We were taught to concentrate on being the best we could be, finding ways to help each other, and discovering our unique identities.

It truly was the healthiest competitive environment I've ever participated in. There was no bickering among the participants. No one tried to sabotage anyone else. I didn't run into any "mind games" where participants might make seemingly benign statements or backhanded compliments designed to shake another participant's confidence.

I placed in the top eight at the Arkansas Junior Miss program but got no further. That surprised me. I really did think I was going to win. After all, why even be there if I didn't expect to win?

I expected success, but my real dream was not to win pageants.

Sure, I enjoyed the process of being in pageants. I liked the public and social world of pageants. I tried to do my best. And I wanted to win, of course. But from my perspective, it was just one more enjoyable activity. My real goal in life was becoming a veterinarian.

There was a high school pageant the next year called the Jonesboro High School Sweetheart pageant. I was elected to participate as a representative of the Future Business Leaders of America. I'm convinced, however, that it was because no one else in our group was willing to do it.

At this point, I'd had enough experience in pageants to have an idea or two about how to handle myself on stage, and so I pretended I was competing in the Miss America pageant.

I mimicked what I had seen on television, specifically how contestants spoke when they were asked questions.

While the other contestants meekly approached the microphone, whispered their names, and mumbled what they wanted to do with their lives, I bounced up to the microphone and said confidently, "Hi! My name is Debbye Turner and I represent the Future Business Leaders of America. I want to be a veterinarian when I grow up and, perhaps, I can be a part of the medical team that finds the cure for cancer!" My gusto and enthusiasm must have made a favorable impression on the judges.

Though it was by all accounts a minor competition, I had developed a new presence on stage. And I won.

In your pursuit of success, never take for granted the experience you gain from things you might not value so highly. Don't despise small beginnings.

I didn't realize it then, but this modest high school pageant—a small competition compared to what lay ahead—was life-shaping. In that moment I literally found my voice in speaking from a platform.

My experiences in pageant competitions at that early time in my life were not vitally important to me. They were never my ultimate goal in life. It was a life I had fallen into, a life that, as a teenage girl, was exciting and just plain fun.

What I didn't understand yet was how these local and regional competitions would give me skills and

> What are the "little things" in your life right now that are seemingly insignificant? Are there learning experiences in them for you? Are they opportunities for developing knowledge and skills?
>
> What might these "insignificant" experiences lead to?

abilities and confidence for what was to come. Not only what was to come in future competitions, but what was to come later in my life.

A surprising result came about from that seemingly inconsequential victory in the Jonesboro High School Sweetheart pageant.

One of the judges, Maxine Hahn, was the director for the Miss Jonesboro pageant, which was a preliminary competition in the Miss America pageant system. She was impressed with me and a few other contestants and extended a personal invitation to compete in Miss Jonesboro.

I really didn't know much about the Miss America pageant, other than what I had seen on television. Mimicking a Miss America contestant while competing in a school pageant was vastly different than believing I could actually compete in Miss America. Frankly, what I'd seen on those annual telecasts was fun to watch, but not particularly relatable to me. For the most part, there were few women of color. No one looked like me on that stage. With their megawatt smiles, big hair, and fancy evening gowns, Miss America contestants seemed like aliens from another planet. I had no reason to believe that I would fit in that culture or that being in that world was even an available option.

Maxine Hahn was persistent. She told me everything that the pageant would offer: I could develop poise and self-esteem, elegance, confidence, and goal-setting skills. That was all very nice, and I had enjoyed the pageants I had competed in, but I had no intention of becoming a professional pageant participant. I thanked her but politely declined, thinking I already had plenty on my plate.

But for some reason, this kind woman was determined to recruit me. She simply refused to take no for an answer.

And then she mentioned that the Miss America organization is one of the largest sources of scholarships for women.

I could possibly be awarded tens of thousands of dollars in scholarship money.

Well, *that* got my attention!

For most of my life I had dreamt of going to veterinary school, but I was well aware that my lower-middle-class family couldn't afford to pay for it. I would have to find ways to cover the expenses: scholarships, loans, a job, whatever means were available. Bells started ringing in my head at the thought of winning scholarship money by competing in the Miss America system. Suddenly, I realized it could be my ticket to paying for veterinary school!

Enthusiastic and excited about this new opportunity to reach my goals, I entered the Miss Jonesboro pageant for the first time at age sixteen. I grew up believing that I could ask God for the desire of my heart, so I prayed for His blessing, favor, and anointing—and that I would win!

Even at that age I had faith that with God anything was possible.

I wish I could say I sensed some higher call in that moment—that I knew God had a life-changing purpose and destiny for my participation in pageants. But I can't.

Most of us lack such insight in the pivotal moments of our lives. We like to think that God will shout from the heavens or speak through a burning bush. But God almost never tells us everything we want to know when we want to know it. He wants us to learn to respond to His voice and trust Him completely as He guides us step by step.

> Who has God put in your path today? Who is walking with you on your journey toward achievement and success?

God did not audibly speak to me that day and say, "Thou shalt be Miss America!" He didn't provide automatic success.

But He did provide Maxine Hahn. I believe it was Maxine Hahn who pointed me down the path God had chosen for me.

I think sometimes the guidance God has for us comes through a person He puts in our path. Success often comes to us through others.

You may not recognize that person at the time but the key is to be open to what God is doing in your life. Be open to those He is using to guide you. This is easier said than done, of course. But prayer and faith will keep you moving in the right direction.

I entered Miss Jonesboro with great expectation.

I had been told by friends and pageant advisors not only that I had great potential and could win but also that I *would* win!

Every time I entered a pageant my family gathered for prayer. I can remember my mother praying for me—that I would do well, that God would give me favor with the judges, and that the light of Jesus would shine through me as a testimony to the other girls. I too would pray and ask God for His blessing—*and that I would win.*

In fact, I wound up in third place.

The first runner-up and the winner were older than me, and much more experienced and mature. People told me that getting second runner-up was quite an accomplishment for a sixteen-year-old, and that I just needed to wait until I was a little older and try again.

I put on a game face and made the best of the outcome, but I was disappointed. My ultimate goal of a veterinary education and winning money to pay my way was thwarted. At least for now.

I couldn't be aware of it yet as a teenager, but I was learning a few lessons. It would take a while before they sunk in, before they became painful enough for me to take notice, but they were there in that experience of losing.

The first lesson is that God doesn't always give us what we want. I thought getting involved in the Miss America program was only a means to an end—a way for me to achieve my primary goal of becoming a veterinarian.

But God had a higher purpose in mind. He had an amazing, and sometimes excruciating, journey planned for my life that would lead me to what He really wanted for me. I neither imagined the long, difficult road that was ahead, nor comprehended the far-reaching consequences of that simple decision. The girl I was then could not have envisioned everything God had planned for me.

How about you? Are you disappointed that what you've been seeking has been thwarted by failure? Have you gotten to a roadblock in your path? Has God not given you the success you asked for?

The good news is that God has a higher purpose for you and that it will be amazing. The not-so-good news is that the journey He has planned for you may very well be hard at times.

Understand that, as you discover your passions and establish your goals in life, the journey will get harder. The competition you face in any area of pursuit will become tougher.

And your failures will feel larger.

As I would soon find out.

The world of pageants can be dizzying to those outside it. In the Miss America system, numerous pageants at local and state levels are entryways to the national competition. In my late teenage years I competed in a number of pageants at the local level with an eye on getting to the stage for Miss Arkansas, the stepping-stone to Miss America.

I tried again in the Miss Jonesboro pageant, this time placing second. Then I competed in the Miss Arkansas State University pageant, which I won.

At the age of nineteen, I was on my way to the Miss Arkansas pageant.

At the time, I still didn't have any realistic expectations for winning the title. The Miss Arkansas pageant was a highly competitive environment. Many of the contestants had been competing in pageants since their toddler years. Most former Miss Arkansas winners had competed for many years in the system before actually winning the title.

Some spent small fortunes on costumes, coaching, trainers, and designer evening gowns. At that point, my costumes were homemade or rented. We couldn't afford coaches and trainers. I was just doing the best I could with the little I had. But my competitive nature made me *want* to win—to do whatever it was going to take to be successful. At the same time, I was simply happy to be there because I had tried for so long to reach that level.

I didn't win.

Considering the stiff competition and highly experienced contestants in the Miss Arkansas pageant, I wasn't very surprised. I was simply no match for the top contenders who were older, more sophisticated, and far better dressed than me. I made the top ten, and once again was told this was good for a nineteen-year-old first-timer at the Miss Arkansas pageant, competing with women in their early twenties.

So I switched tactics.

I decided to stop competing and wait until I was a couple of years older and possessed the same maturity and experience of those other women. I didn't have any aspirations of becoming

Miss America at that point. I just wanted to be Miss Arkansas. The new Miss Arkansas would get a fur coat, a new car to drive for a year, and a generous scholarship to go toward her education.

That all sounded really good.

Two years later, at twenty-one years old, I won another local pageant and returned to the Miss Arkansas stage. This time I was serious. I was older, and more of a veteran of pageants. I knew what to expect. I had been there before, and I now was prepared. I had sought the advice of everyone I could think of.

I really wanted to win, and I was driven to put in the work I needed to.

For the talent portion, I was playing the marimba. I'd been developing my music skills for a number of years, but now I practiced three hours every day, taking private lessons to sharpen my skills. And I was a member of the percussion section of the Arkansas State University marching band.

A part of the Miss America competition is a private, job-style interview. Contestants are asked all sorts of questions, including about the world around us. I wanted to make sure that I was impeccably prepared for every possible question. To hone my interview skills, I voraciously read newspapers and news magazines and incessantly watched newscasts. I took notes on current events and social issues, then spent time thinking about my opinions and perspectives on those issues. I had a huge three-ring binder notebook in which I kept notes on current events, social issues, and my thoughts about world affairs. I asked local business professionals and my mother's friends to conduct mock interviews. They did, firing all sorts of questions at me. At the end of each, they critiqued my answers. Sometimes we even videotaped the interviews. I watched them repeatedly, trying to master my answers, posture, and facial expressions.

Next, I had to improve my onstage walk. My ballet teacher and family friend, Sylvia Richards, once told me that I walked like a goat. As harsh as that sounds, it was what I needed to hear. And work on. Again, we could not afford special trainers or coaches, so I had to teach myself. I practiced in the unfinished basement of our home, empty except for our washing machine and dryer, a few boxes, and items tucked away for storage. Propping up a full-length mirror, I walked back and forth in front of it—sometimes for hours—wearing high heels, practicing my posture and carriage. I practiced my turn, smile, and the way I tilted my head as I made the turn.

I was extremely focused and left nothing to chance. In my mind, when I arrived at the Miss Arkansas pageant, I was there to do a job. While I did want to have fun and enjoy the experience, I was not there to make friends or be elected Miss Congeniality. I had dedicated time and preparation to compete successfully in all areas of competition and I intended to do so. Making friends would be the icing on the cake.

As it turned out, I didn't get the cake or the icing.

I placed first runner-up to the new Miss Arkansas. Second place.

Devastated, I decided that it just must not be God's will for me to win Miss Arkansas and go on to the Miss America pageant, because if it was, I would have won. It was 1986 and I was in my second year of veterinary school. I decided I could continue to finance my education through guaranteed student loans like many other students. I didn't need this pageant stuff. So, I announced to everyone that I was going to quit.

My pageant life was finished!

In that moment, I made two mistakes. One was that I let failure defeat me and destroy my dream. In fact, I'd had some wins in my pageant career. But there were a lot of runners-up. And this prize of winning Miss Arkansas had eluded me a second time. Now I was giving in to the disappointment of failure and throwing in the towel.

I told myself that the whole experience had been a positive one; after all, it had been enjoyable, I had earned a measure of success, and I had won some scholarship money along the way. Now it was time to give it all up, I told myself.

The *real* reason I was making this decision was that I was disappointed, even frustrated, with my efforts.

My second mistake was that *I* made the decision to quit. Never once had I asked God what *He* wanted me to do—I didn't consult Him about getting into pageants and I didn't consult Him about getting out of them.

Does this sound familiar? Is this true of something in your life right now? How often do we choose to do something with our own agenda and then get disappointed when God doesn't fulfill our expectations? Too often to count, based on my personal experience.

> What have you chosen to do with your own agenda and then been disappointed when God didn't fulfill your expectations?

Thankfully, God doesn't let us off so easily. He doesn't let go of the dream He has for you and me.

Now finished competing, I concentrated solely on completing my education and doing other things I enjoyed.

But people came into my life to speak to me, saying things like, "Debbye, I don't believe God would have you settle for second best" and "So, Debbye, what is *God's* will in these pageants?" I hadn't really considered that before, but it didn't really matter—I had made up my mind, and that was that!

During this time, my mother was holding an intercessory prayer meeting in our home on Saturday mornings. At one session, my mom's dear friend, Dorothy Brown, shared with me a vision she'd had: "Debbye, I saw you with a white gown on and a crown on your head and roses in your hand," she said. "I believe if you don't quit, God will elevate you to the top. You are not supposed to give up!"

That shook me. God had my attention.

I began earnestly praying about what God wanted me to do in these pageants—not just, *I'm gonna do these pageants, so bless me, Lord, and help me win!* As I sought the Lord for His will and guidance, I began to believe I shouldn't quit, because God had a purpose for my participation.

"OK, Lord," I said. "I gave it my very best the first two times at the Miss Arkansas pageant and that wasn't good enough to win. You want me to do this and so you need to show me how. You teach me how."

It was time to get back in the game.

In 1987, I entered a local pageant, Miss Red River Valley, and again placed second. Ugh. I felt I would forever be Miss First Runner-Up.

A few weeks later, I entered another local pageant, Miss Northeast Arkansas, and this time I won, which led to my competing in the Miss Arkansas pageant for the third time.

This time everyone expected me to win. I had finished first runner-up the previous year at Miss Arkansas, so I returned as the favorite and I was ready to win. I was more mature, had the pageant thing down cold, people were praying for me, *and* for the first time I had an overwhelming sense that this wasn't just my own thing, but it was what God wanted for me.

I believed, in fact, God put people around me as special provision.

When God has a plan for us, He doesn't just tell us, "Go do this the best way you know how." Instead, He provides the way. When He has a purpose for our lives, He also makes the provision for that purpose!

My experience with selecting an evening gown is a good example.

I met a local clothing designer, Tim Cobb, who agreed to help me design just the right evening gown for the Miss Arkansas competition. This was the late 1980s and shiny, beaded evening gowns with giant shoulder pads were all the rage. Designers Bob Mackey and Stephen Yearick dominated the fashion runways. Well, I certainly couldn't afford one of their gowns; they cost thousands of dollars. They were so expensive because the fabric was hand-beaded.

I couldn't afford one, but I *really* wanted that edge.

God made a way! If I could supply the beaded fabric, Tim agreed to design and make the evening gown at a cost that was affordable for my family. So I recruited a couple of my friends and we sat in a back room of Tim's shop and painstakingly sewed the beads on the fabric by hand, one bead at a time.

There could be as many as a thousand beads in just a square foot of material. My fingers cramped. At times, my vision got blurry from focusing on the tiny beads for so long. The fabric was stretched tight on a frame, similar to the way a painter's canvas stretches over a frame. My neck and back knotted painfully from bending over the frame for hours at a time.

I sewed beads in the evenings, on weekends, and even between my college classes. It took weeks to complete the countless hours of back-breaking work. But we got it done.

And Tim made the most gorgeous beaded white gown for me to wear during the evening gown competition at the Miss Arkansas pageant.

The weeklong preliminaries went smoothly. I won my talent preliminary and even won the swimsuit preliminary competition, which was a miracle! It was my least favorite part of competing and I did not have the rail-thin figure that was expected at the time. I am naturally curvy, even when thin. Those curves were not appreciated or celebrated. That Saturday night I was named as one of the top ten finalists. Everything went perfectly. I answered my on-stage question well, I didn't trip and fall, and there were no wardrobe malfunctions. I knew I couldn't have done any better. It was finally my time to become Miss Arkansas.

Over the previous years I had developed a little system when the runners-up and winner were announced. While I was standing on stage, right before they called out each runner-up position, I would earnestly and silently pray, *God, don't let that be me!* This year, I prayed again, but my heart was different this time.

The emcee said, "And the third runner-up is," and I prayed silently, *Lord, your will be done.* They called someone else's name and I thought *Whew! Thank You, Lord!* Then the emcee bellowed, "And the second runner-up is . . ." and I prayed silently again, *Lord, your will be done.* They called someone else's name. And finally, the emcee declared, "The first runner-up is . . ."

At this point, I had been first runner-up many, many times on the local level, and the previous year at the Miss Arkansas pageant. I really did *not* enjoy being first runner-up. I would rather be *anything* besides first runner-up. But I had reached the point that I wanted God's will more than I wanted my own. The emcee began the usual speech, "The first runner-up position is very important, because in the event that the winner cannot fulfill her duties, then the first runner-up will step forward" blah, blah, blah.

God, your will be done, I prayed with all my heart as he spoke.

Even though I didn't want to be first runner-up again, I

wanted what God wanted. "And the first runner-up is . . . Debbye Turner."

To say I was shocked would be an understatement. I was convinced that I was going to win. Not out of the place of arrogance or overconfidence. I had worked very hard and prayed and fasted and believed God and thought I'd heard from God. So in my mind, it was established and settled. And I was there to fulfill my divine destiny.

I was mortified, disappointed, and downright heartbroken. But all eyes were on me. People were taking pictures. TV cameras were rolling. So I had to put on a brave face. I plastered on the most authentic smile I could muster. Using proper pageant etiquette and demonstrating good sportsmanship, I turned to the judges who were seated just in front of the stage to my left. I nodded my head and mouthed, "Thank you." Someone brought me a bouquet of roses and a silver tray as tokens of my achievement. Then I was quickly escorted to the side of the stage to make way for the real star of the night, the new Miss Arkansas.

Patti Jo Thorn was the new Miss Arkansas. She was a gifted opera singer, with blonde curls, long legs, and a megawatt smile. I liked Patti Jo. I was even happy for her. But I was stunned that she was wearing "my" crown and Miss Arkansas sash. I just couldn't figure out where it all went wrong.

After the emcees thanked the audience for coming and made a few final comments, the show was over.

And there I stood on the side of the stage, shell-shocked with a smile frozen on my face.

———

That was the most disappointing, devastating moment of my life. I'm here to tell you that if that's where you are right now, if that's the moment you're in, then God has you exactly where He wants you.

In those moments I was confused. And honestly, I cannot say why things happen the way they happen. Why God does things a different way than we expect. We don't always know His purposes. Often we will be confused and disappointed.

I had heard God's call to get back in the game. I had seen His provision for me through people and talents and resources. I had prayed for God's will to be done. I had turned things over to Him. I'd done everything right. I'd given God the key to my success.

Very often our ultimate success comes out of failure. What you and I think of as success in the moment of this endeavor or that project or some dream might not be important in the light of our entire lives, in the full scope of what God knows is important down the road.

The key to success is in failure. Why? Because in our failure we are driven to God. And we are more open to being redirected to His plan and purpose.

My family and friends who'd come to cheer me on that night came up to the stage to congratulate me. But they looked like they were coming to view the dead. They were shocked, disappointed, and, in some cases, angry. Many hugged me and offered half-hearted congratulations.

After the pageant, I asked my family to stay down in the lobby of the hotel where I was staying, and I went up to my room. I just wanted to be alone. I barely made it inside the door before I fell to the floor heaving with sobs. Curled up in the fetal position, I cried my heart out. All my frustration and disappointment, not only from this outcome, but from so many other pageants that I'd been disappointed in, flowed out of me in a torrent of tears.

But finally I quieted enough to hear God speak to my heart, *Debbye, I'm faithful. Now get up.*

I had a choice: to believe Him—or my situation. I chose to believe God.

In that moment, I didn't know how but I knew with absolute certainty that God was going to perform His word to me. He had demonstrated His faithfulness over and over in my life, as far back as I could remember. I had watched Him provide finances as my mother struggled to raise two girls by herself. I had watched Him heal us when my mom prayed for us when we were sick. I had experienced His protection when we didn't even know we were in danger until it had already passed.

I wasn't going to give up because I had a vision of something eternal. My competing was no longer a little after-school hobby. It was no longer about the thrill and accolades of winning. It was no longer about the kick I got out of the acceptance and applause. It was, for the very first time, about what God's purpose was for my life. From that night forward my heart's prayer was, *Lord, I not only want You to be involved in every area of this pageant thing, but whatever Your purpose is in my life, that's what I want.*

With that new vision, I picked myself up off the floor, washed my face, took a shower, put on some comfortable clothes, and went down to have dinner with my family. During dinner, my family and friends made their opinions known—again. My sister and Dad thought that I should quit and move on with my life.

But they were not privy to my hotel-room encounter with God. I was changed, and there was no going back. I didn't immediately know what I was going to do, but I knew I wasn't going to give up. I left dinner determined to trust God. I earnestly started fasting and praying, not just for God's involvement, certainly not only for His blessing, but for His purpose.

33

TWO

Faith

In its purest sense, faith is a decision to believe in something. The question is what we choose to believe in. Everything we do requires faith.

Faith empowers daily living. From getting out of bed in the morning to winning an Olympic gold medal, you cannot know for sure what will happen today or this week or in the years to come.

Conversely, the absence of faith is fear. And your actions reveal if you are driven by faith—or fear.

I believe a shocking number of us give up right when we are on the brink of success. We may not be guaranteed success if we finish. But we are guaranteed failure if we don't finish.

Fear plays a role in failure. But faith is greater than fear, enabling us to pivot from failure to success. It gets us to the finish line.

The COVID-19 pandemic has proven just how uncertain circumstances can be, how quickly the definition of *normal* can change. And how important faith is under all conditions.

Believing in yourself is critical to daily living—and success. You can conduct your life with the *faith* that you can do what you need to do.

I fully accept the importance of having confidence in yourself. But it's interesting that so many who accept the idea of having faith in themselves somehow minimize the idea of faith in God.

Who has most shaped your faith in God, and belief in yourself?

How does their influence aid or hinder your ability to trust that God never fails?

By refocusing from "faith in me" to "faith *first* in God," how might you pursue success differently?

I am alive today because of my mother's prayers. Gussie Turner, my mom, was a woman of great faith who believed in the omnipotent power of an almighty and good God. And while she was in every sense a mere mortal, her faith was unshakable and infectious.

Her faith manifested itself in the form of unceasing and fervent prayer. In our home, prayer was not just an activity. And it certainly was far more than a mealtime ritual called "grace" or an obligatory exercise before we ate. In our home, prayer was *alive*. It was powerful, and effective. And I experienced that power on full display in our lives. My mother believed and expected that, when she prayed, things would happen.

And did she ever pray!

We prayed together as a family every day. Before we left the house, we gathered in a circle, held hands, and prayed as my mom asked God to orchestrate our day. She prayed for protection, wisdom, and blessings. She was very careful to acknowledge the Lord before starting *any* day.

Nonetheless, mornings were a harried, sometimes chaotic time in the Turner household. In the mad dash to get up and dressed, eat breakfast, fix lunch, *and* gather our homework and after-school gear, we frequently ran late. It never failed that on the days we were the tardiest, just as we would fly out the door to jump in the car, my mother realized that she didn't know where she had left the car keys. We put down backpacks, lunch boxes, and whatever else filled our arms and searched the house for the car keys. As I looked behind pillows, under chairs, and on counters, I could hear my mom praying.

"Lord, help us find the keys. Come out, keys, in the name of Jesus!"

No sooner than she made her bold proclamation, one of us would stumble upon the keys. And out the door we raced, grateful and late.

At other points in my childhood, I thought my mom might pray my older sister and me to death. We prayed about *everything*. Had a test at school? "Let's pray!" Competing in a band competition? "Let's pray!" Needing money for a field trip? "Let's pray!" What should I wear to give my class speech? "Let's pray about it and see what the Lord says!"

Although prayer was a lifestyle—and lifeline—I often wondered why we needed to bother a surely busy God with such mundane requests. A big, holy God couldn't possibly be interested in everyday drama, right?

Actually, wrong. He cares about *everything* that concerns us.

Eventually, I understood that my mom was determined to teach me that God dwells in the details. He even cared about the minutiae of *my* life. My mom often declared, "God even knows the very number of hairs on your head," a reference to Matthew 10:30. So we prayed a lot. She taught me that prayer is a tool for survival.

I still start my days with prayer. No matter how early I rise or how busy the day, the moment I open my eyes, I thank God for another day and ask for wisdom to get me through whatever life will bring. When we do this—acknowledge the Lord—He promises to direct our path (Proverbs 3:6).

When I was just a tyke, I struggled with fear of the dark. I was convinced that monsters lived in my closet and in the shadows of my bedroom. I was terrified, too afraid to even get up and run to my mom's room for comfort. From time to time, I wet the bed because I was too frightened to sneak past those imaginary apparitions to get to the bathroom!

One morning after Mommy discovered my pee-stained sheets, she asked in exasperation why I didn't simply get up and go to the bathroom. I finally divulged that I was afraid of "the witch." I explained she was an ugly, old lady with a hooked nose that had a wart on its end. Wrapped in a shawl, she sat in a rocking chair at the foot of my bed. (Forty-five years later, I still remember her—vividly!)

She wasn't real, of course, but my fear was. I was too scared to get up, so I lay there until I just couldn't keep my bladder in check. Mommy told me that I had authority in the name of Jesus, and that perfect love casts out all fear. She taught me that I could rebuke the enemy in Jesus's name and command him to flee. So after that incident, whenever something scared me or I thought I saw giant, hairy ghouls lurking under the bed, I yelled, "Get out of here, in Jesus's name!"

And you know what? Everything would be OK. From then on, whenever I was fearful about anything, I prayed as my mother had taught me. I rebuked the enemy and asked for God's grace and help. Whether I felt immediate peace or not, I had an assurance that God heard my prayers and was protecting me.

My mom and dad were a power couple long before power couples were a thing.

Frederick Cornelius Turner Jr., my dad, is *literally* tall, dark, and handsome. At six foot one, he has soft, wavy hair; bright, playful eyes; and a smile that could light up New York City's

Times Square. He has a magnetic, charismatic personality. I have never in my life met anyone who doesn't like him. He lights up a room when he enters. He laughs easily and heartily. He has a wicked—even naughty—sense of humor. And he loves nothing more than telling stories, playing games, and just being with friends and family.

Although my mother, Gussie Lee Jones, later developed into a true force of nature, when she was younger the family lore is that she was quiet and demure. She was absolutely gorgeous. She had buttery smooth, caramel-colored skin, dreamy eyes, and a supermodel smile. And she was a statuesque five foot ten and built like the proverbial brick house. Kind and compassionate, she was quick to go out of her way to help others.

My parents knew each other as children. My dad grew up in Jonesboro, Arkansas. My mother grew up in Kennett, Missouri, about an hour's drive away. Mommy spent summers in Jonesboro with her aunt, Anita Berry. That's how my parents met. They played together as kids in the hot, sticky Arkansas heat. One summer, when my mom returned to Jonesboro for her annual summer visit, she was different. Puberty was doing its mysterious work. No longer the chubby-cheeked little girl with stubby pigtails, she was tall and curvy, and far more interesting to my dad. They soon began to date. They married when my mom was twenty-one years old and my dad twenty-three.

My father had graduated from Arkansas State University and was a commissioned officer in the United States Army. Eventually he would do three tours in Vietnam. I am so very proud of his sacrifice and dedication.

In 1961, my mom and dad welcomed my sister and only sibling, Suzette, into their lives. My parents moved to Honolulu, Hawaii, where my dad was stationed. On September 19, 1965, I was born. To this day, I love claiming Hawaii as my birthplace. We moved away to my dad's next military assignment just months after I was born. Thus, I have no memory of living in Hawaii—but I love having the bragging rights.

In 1969, Arkansas State University (ASU) recruited my father to join the staff of its Reserved Officer Training Corps (ROTC) Department. This was historic: my father became the first African American to teach on ASU's staff.

We lived in campus housing a short while, but soon my parents were renovating my father's childhood home that he had inherited from his mom when she died from brain cancer. We moved there when I was five. It had a huge backyard. The neighborhood was a close-knit community where everyone looked out for each other. We knew all the families who lived on our block. And although the neighborhood was predominantly White, with the exception of our family and the families on either side of us, everyone seemed to get along well. My childhood up to this point was idyllic, or so I thought.

I didn't know it at the time, but my parents' marriage was crumbling.

I remember the talk that my dad had with my sister and me to tell us that he would be moving out. He sat in "his chair" in our living room. A black leather recliner with an ottoman, it seemed to be big enough to cradle the whole world. It held me, my dolls, and one or two of our cats. I could crawl up in it and play for hours. But it also seemed exotic and forbidden because when my dad was around, no one could sit there. That was his throne. He read the newspaper, took naps, watched TV, and on that memorable day he delivered life-altering news from it.

My sister and I sat across from him with wide eyes and anticipation. I didn't know what was about to happen, but I could tell that it was something important. *Maybe I'm finally getting that pony I always wanted.*

My father drew in a deep breath. I could see faint tears glistening in the corner of his eyes. He seemed sad, but I couldn't imagine why. *Ponies aren't sad*, I thought.

He told us that he loved us very much and was so proud to be our father. He then explained that he and my mom were not getting along and that he was moving out of our home. By this time his tears flowed freely. My sister cried too. Although I heard his words, I didn't fully understand their implication. I got that he was moving out. But that wasn't all bad—in my mind.

My father was, and still is, an old-school military man. He was raised with, and lived out, very traditional patriarchal values. He believed that a wife's place was in the home. He thought that a woman's duty was to raise the children, keep a nice home, and cook delicious three-course meals. Daddy came home from work every day expecting a "proper" dinner on the table. For me, that was a drag.

I often wanted pizza, hot dogs, or even fish sticks for dinner. But those were not appropriate dinner fare in our household. So my mom served a meat, vegetable (*yuck!*), and starch for every dinner. That was the rule. When my father tearfully announced that he was moving out, my first thought was, *All right! We get to have pizza for dinner now!*

It's amazing how a five-year-old processes tragedy.

And it's amazing how tragedy brings people back to God.

When their marriage began to fall apart, my mom recommitted her life to the Lord. She had grown up in the church and gave her heart to the Lord as a teenager but wandered away from her relationship with God as a young adult.

Now faced with becoming a single parent and having to provide for her daughters in a way which she was not equipped to do at the time, she sought God for direction and wisdom.

I observed her spiritual growth without realizing then the significance of what I was seeing. I remember being around six or seven years old when I saw my mother pray and read the Bible more. We started going to revivals and prayer meetings, sometimes driving hundreds of miles to hear a popular preacher or attend a church conference. My mom was hungry to know the Bible better and experience more of God in her daily life.

One day when I was around ten years old, my mother announced that she wanted to know God better and live a more anointed life. So she decided to go on a forty-day fast, just like Moses and Jesus did in the Bible. She believed that it would increase her intimacy with God. So she stopped eating solid food for forty days. As I remember it, she only drank water. Life, for me, didn't change.

And at first, it didn't seem to change for my mom either. She continued to work, cook dinner, and pray for people. But as the fast progressed, her energy began to wane. When she couldn't keep up her hectic daily schedule, she asked my grandmother to come stay with us and take over caring for my sister and me. My mom then went into her bedroom and closed the door. She didn't come out for more than a week, except to use the bathroom. I was not allowed to go into the bedroom to visit her, and was never sure what was happening behind that closed door. But I could hear her through the door praying, worshipping, and singing to God, even sometimes crying. She wanted more of God. I wasn't really concerned through all this because my grandmother was with us. All of our needs were met, and she spoiled us.

I remember very clearly the end of my mom's fast. After the fortieth day, she opened the door and came out of the bedroom. She looked like a different person. While she was slimmer, she did not look gaunt, or weak, or sad after going for more than a month with no food. Her eyes were bright like car headlights. Her skin seemed to glow and shimmer. The biggest smile I'd ever seen on her lit her countenance. To me, it looked like a white light surrounded her. She was changed.

I didn't understand it then, but looking back I realize that, after that forty-day fast, life in the Turner household also changed. That's when my mom started praying about *every-thing*. That's when the Thursday night Bible prayer groups began. That's when I started seeing people, including myself, change as a result of my mother's prayers.

———

People flocked to our home because they needed prayer support—and more faith for everyday living. My mother set the example that prayer is for the big and the small things. God cares about our cares (1 Peter 5:7).

One thing we all tend to get wrong is the idea that true success in life is about smooth sailing. We somehow expect things to go well, and when they don't, we crumble.

As a girl of five encountering the divorce of my parents, I would only think about pizza for dinner. I didn't know enough about adversity then. But looking back on that time, I see my mom with new eyes. She faced the huge and painful loss of her marriage with courage and determination.

And it was through turning to faith in God.

Winning in life doesn't happen only when there is smooth sailing. We don't achieve success just when things are easy. We succeed not in spite of obstacles but because of them.

The traumas and tragedies of life are what give us the very things that equip us for the achievement.

And the secret for overcoming the hard times is our faith in God.

———

My mother's desire, even desperation, to know God more changed her life, our family, and the lives of countless other people.

As my mother grew spiritually, so did I. She was learning

to pray more effectively, live more purposefully, and trust God implicitly. She taught me the importance of spiritual growth through the example she set, a growth that started with faith. If prayer was the air we breathed, faith was the food we ate. We couldn't live without either. When facing hardships, the first thing we did was pray. Following that, we exercised our faith by declaring the promises of God found in the Bible.

Because she was a single mom, days were full and exhausting. Very often, the first quiet moments my mom had to herself occurred at night, after my sister and I had gone to bed. Her prayers filled the house—and our ears.

It was in those late-night hours that I heard my mom praying, sincerely and sometimes urgently. She was not a quiet pray-er. There were times her loud cries to the Father would awaken me. I tried muffling her prayers by covering my head with my pillow or putting my fingers in my ears. Nothing worked. After a while I learned to lie there and pray along with my mom. I also silently asked God to hear her prayers so she would stop and I could get some sleep. Sleep was not always possible, because during those nightly marathon prayer sessions, my mom frequently woke us up to join her in prayer.

"Get up! God wants us to pray," she insisted, flipping on the overhead light.

Needless to say, I was not as enthusiastic as my mom. I would drag myself out of my warm bed and we would assemble at our usual prayer location: the hallway outside our bedrooms. There, we would stand in a circle, holding hands as my mother called down heaven. And we were expected to join in.

Just standing with our eyes closed as she prayed was not an option. She believed—and taught us—that prayer is a team effort, not a spectator sport. So she expected us to pray and agree along with her. If she didn't hear an occasional "Yes, Lord" or "Thank you, Jesus!" out of us, she scolded us. So

I taught myself to sleep standing up, rousing myself every so often to mumble a "Yes, Lord" just to stay out of trouble.

I didn't understand it then, but I know *now* that my mother was teaching me a prayer ethic. Prayer should be a lifestyle. It is greatly underutilized if it's just something we occasionally do when life gets hard. Rather, I have discovered it is as elemental to our life, faith, and survival as air, food, and water.

I believe prayer was not burdensome for me as a child because I had already put my trust in God. I came to accept Jesus as my Savior at age seven. It was not at church or in Sunday school. I heard the gospel of Jesus Christ sitting at our kitchen table.

Back then, in my town, children learned the alphabet in first grade and didn't learn to read until second grade. I walked the two blocks to and from school every day. My mom would stand at our side door, watching me walk home each afternoon. "How was school?" she would ask. When I entered second grade, my mom started asking daily, "Can you read a sentence yet?"

I thought this was an odd question to ask, especially every day, but I assumed that as soon as I could read a full sentence that some delicious treat or great reward would follow. That day finally arrived.

I ran down the big hill on Cherry Street toward our house, screaming at the top of my lungs. Excited, I could barely stay on my feet as I tore through the neighbor's backyard, under our carport, up the steps, and in the side door.

"Mommy, I can read! I can read a full sentence!"

I repeated myself as if she hadn't heard me for the last two blocks. She'd walked away from the door and sat at our breakfast table in the kitchen. When I looked over to see her, I was bursting with anticipation. I didn't know what reward I'd receive for my momentous milestone, but I knew it had to be good considering my mom had inquired about my reading ability for so long. She called me over to the table and pointed to a chair. I was too excited to sit down, but I obeyed.

"Sweetheart, you can't get to heaven on my apron string," she said with a loving, all-enveloping smile.

I didn't quite know what she meant by this, but I listened carefully, waiting to hear what prize was in store.

"You must know God for yourself," she said. "You must be able to pray on your own. And you have to read the Bible for yourself."

Okay. What does this have to do with my prize?

Oblivious to my thoughts, she pointed at the book in front of her. I hadn't noticed it before.

"The only way to really get to know God is by reading this . . . the Bible. This is your very own Bible," she said, pushing it toward me. "Read it every day, for the rest of your life," she solemnly instructed.

That was it? That was my big surprise?

Thoughts churning, I sat motionless for a second. *Where's my reward for learning to read? Why are we talking about the Bible?*

This didn't make sense. Then she showed me Scriptures that explained how I could be saved. She explained that *saved* meant believing that Jesus is the Son of God, and that Jesus died for my sins. That it meant accepting His work of salvation, thereby saving my soul from eternal damnation, giving me the right to eternal life with God in heaven, and enabling me through the Holy Spirit to follow the teachings of Christ in my daily life. Then she asked me if I was ready to ask Jesus to "come into my heart."

By this time, I had figured out there was no treat. At least not the kind I was expecting. I also knew that I wanted to go to heaven. I wanted to have this Jesus in my heart like I saw demonstrated in my mom's life.

"Yes, I want to be saved," I admitted.

And right there at our kitchen table, Mommy prayed a prayer of salvation with me. I didn't know then how revolutionary it would be in my life. I did not know I had just received the ultimate prize; my understanding of that moment would grow and evolve over time. But, despite not receiving a treat or gift for learning to read, I was happy. Happier than I'd ever been.

It was in that kitchen moment that I first tasted what faith in God is. I wouldn't know for some years faith's role in empowering me to live the life God purposed for me. And in my teenage years, through my pageant competitions, I had to learn, sometimes painfully, what faith is and isn't, how God's desire for me isn't always what my desire is. I am still discovering the many dimensions of what faith in God really means.

But that moment with Mommy was the foundation for the faith in God that has guided me all my life.

I believe I was blessed to come to God when I was a child. But it doesn't matter at what time of life you come to God. The point is that faith in God can lead to unexplainable joy and fulfillment. We are fulfilled not by what we want but by what God wants for us. There is a higher level of joy when we live the life that God wants for us, beyond what we want for ourselves. When we define true success from God's perspective, we win, every time!

In many ways after that day, life went on as it had before I became a Christian. I went to school. I came home and played. I did chores. And I began to read the Bible. Really, the only Scripture passage that I could find that made any sense at all to me was Psalm 23. I must have read that chapter a thousand times, mainly because I didn't know what else to read. But the richness and mystery of the Bible blossomed in my heart. In addition to the many daily family prayers I endured, I started to develop my own prayer life, without my mom.

I started praying about my own concerns, big or small. I prayed to ask God to help me with my schoolwork. I prayed for protection when I went for a bike ride or walked to a different neighborhood. I also prayed about my future; who I was supposed to be when I grew up, who I was supposed to marry.

I remember once, when I was around twelve, I went to Mommy and complained that I didn't have a best friend. While I got along with most of my schoolmates, there was no one I could confide in or share secrets with. I felt lonely and out of place. When I poured my heart out to my mother about this state of despair, I really wanted her comfort and sympathy.

I wanted her to take me in her arms and tell me how special and beautiful I was, and then maybe give me a yummy treat or cook my favorite meal. Basically, I wanted her to act like the mom on *The Brady Bunch*, one of my all-time favorite TV sitcoms.

After listening intently to my complaint, she advised, "Pray about it. God will send you a best friend."

What? I thought. *That's all you got? Pray about it?*

I left the conversation frustrated and unfulfilled.

Nonetheless, when my mother suggested that I pray for a best friend—even though it sounded religious and irrelevant at the time—I prayed.

"God, please give me a best friend."

I went on with my day and gave my prayer very little thought. But it wasn't long before I discovered Mom's advice was golden, and God had heard my request. Within a week or two, a new family moved to town. One of my mother's friends called, informing her that this new family had daughters and was wondering if my mom would let me play with them. One of the daughters was just a year older than me. We hit it off right away, becoming fast friends. *Best* friends. Look at that: God answered a lonely preteen's prayer. And with that experience, I began to understand the power of a sincere request, prayed in faith, even when uttered by a child.

My mom started a weekly Bible study in our home that eventually became known as the "Thursday Night Share Group." At first, a handful of mostly young women gathered in our living room to listen to my mom teach the Bible, to learn to pray, and to hear from God. It wasn't long before our small living room was jam-packed with people from all walks of life; parents, young adults, students, community leaders, and professors came to hear the Word of God.

We brought the dining room chairs into the living room to accommodate our guests. When we ran out of chairs, my mom sewed large bean bag chairs. After a while, the living room could no longer hold the crowd. People sat or stood everywhere—in corners, down the hallway, in the dining room, and even back into the kitchen. They came not just because my mother was a great Bible teacher (which she was!), but because their lives were changing for the better as they learned what the Bible says about who God is and who we are in God.

During those meetings, I watched the power of God come alive. Most of what I know about God and the Bible I learned while sitting in on those Thursday Night Share Groups. And let me make it clear, they were not optional for me. My mom required that I attend every week. But I didn't mind; her command of God's Word was awesome and encouraged my continued spiritual growth throughout life. Home is where I learned that God loves me just as I am; that Jesus died for my sins; that because of Christ's death, I can live a victorious life forgiven of my sins and free from damnation. I also saw the gifts of the Holy Spirit in operation.

And that is another reason people crowded into our home. People were hungry for proof that God could and would answer prayer. They received this teaching in our living room. Every week, a time of prayer and intercession followed the Bible lesson. My mom placed a dining room chair in the middle of the room and invited anyone who had a prayer request or needed God to intervene in their lives to sit in the "prayer chair." Everybody then encircled that person and prayed.

My mother firmly believed in the power of prayer. For others, perhaps their walk with God is more focused on reading the Bible, say, or going to church. My mom taught me that prayer is a lifeline and key to a relationship with God.

At those weekly sessions, my mom taught us that our own ordinary words reach the ears of our extraordinary God. There is no need for fanfare or pomp. Simply put, prayer is communicating with the God of the universe who also is *that* Good Friend who wholeheartedly cares about you and me.

I have found prayer to God, in faith, to be essential to a relationship with Him. By bringing yourself into the presence of God, you hear His heart and can receive guidance for the pursuit of your dreams.

Like other families, we went to church every Sunday. We were members of St. Paul African Methodist Episcopal Church, the church my father grew up in. But its weekly hour or so service was just the beginning of churchgoing for us. We also attended the evening service at the local "holiness" church, where the high-spirited (and long!) services included testimonies where people stood up and shared how God had blessed them recently; seemingly never-ending intercessory prayer; and call-down-heaven-drive-the-devil-to-hell sermons—all capped off with one or more people jumping, shouting, and running up and down the aisles.

I was never frightened by all the emotional displays and spiritual happenings. Actually, in my childish thinking, I sometimes found the service highly entertaining. My friends and I laid odds on which lady would "shout" her wig off first, which man might take off running across the front of the church first, or which newly converted person might swoon under the Spirit's power—or fall out on the floor. We kids thought church was better than TV!

I am not exaggerating when I say that we went to church every time the doors opened. Bible studies, worship services, special programs, prayer meetings, revivals, and conferences filled our lives. There was a time when we joined a church in Memphis, Tennessee, an hour's drive from Jonesboro. We took that drive as often as four times a week for services, conferences, and meetings. Attending church was a lifestyle.

Oddly enough, though, by the time I was about fifteen years old, I operated under a strict separation of church and school. At school, I was a percussionist in the band, a top-ranked snare drummer in our state. I was a straight-A student and involved in several clubs at school. I was called "gifted and talented" and was invited to attend an exclusive summer educational retreat called Governor's School. I was the only African American in the gifted and talented program in my grade at Jonesboro High School.

I stayed out of trouble, mostly. I also pretended to be cool and hip like I perceived the popular kids were. I just wanted to be liked and accepted . . . by everybody. So I altered my behavior slightly depending on which group of kids I hung with, desperately trying to fit in. I knew being a "church girl" was not the way to do so. Therefore, I didn't talk about God or my faith at school. I didn't mention that I spent practically my whole weekend in church. I certainly didn't want to be branded a "holy roller." The last thing I wanted to be at school was different, so I put on an act. Few of my classmates knew I was a Christian.

In effect, I lived a double life. While I didn't party or drink or do drugs, I also was not a "city set on a hill" (as in Matthew 5:14) when it came to my faith in Jesus. I just never bothered to talk about God at school, so when one of my best buddies saw me at a city-wide church youth revival and was shocked to see me there, I knew something needed to change.

One of the larger White churches hosted the revival, which was announced at my school and around town. Free pizza drew me to the event, or so I thought.

God had bigger plans. I don't remember many of the details of the service, but I do remember how the evening started and how it ended for me.

When I walked into the church before the service started, I immediately saw one of my marching band mates.

"Debbye, what are you doing here?" she asked, incredulous.

Without thinking, I replied, "I came to hear the preacher like everyone else."

"Are *you* a Christian?"

"Yes! Of course I am," I blurted.

I went on to tell her how often I went to church and how much my family prayed. She was not impressed. While I was trying to convince her of my great faith, something my mother had always said finally made sense. At times when I tried pleading my case with my mom after some wrongdoing, she shook her head and said, "Uh, uh, uh. I can't hear what you're saying because what you're doing is talking too loudly."

That never made any sense to me, until that moment. Suddenly, I realized that no matter what I said to my friend, my life and behavior said something completely different. I had been ashamed of my Christianity. I had hidden my "light." Now I was ashamed of my hypocrisy.

I no longer remember what the guest preacher said that night. But I do remember thinking how I must have broken God's heart by pretending at school that I didn't know Him. I had known all along that my main purpose as a Christian was to be a witness of the love of God through Christ Jesus, and I'd failed miserably.

At the conclusion of the sermon, the guest preacher extended an invitation for anyone at the service who didn't know Jesus and wanted to invite Him into their heart to come forward. I wanted to make things right with God. I wanted to repent for leading a double life. But the invitation was not for me. I had accepted Jesus into my heart eight years earlier at my family's kitchen table. Then the guest preacher made a second invitation. He invited those who had a relationship with Jesus but had drifted away from Him to come forward to recommit their lives to God. *Bingo!* I thought, *that's for me.*

Still, I hesitated. I wanted to recommit my life to Jesus. But I wrestled with being rejected by my friends. I was afraid of being teased about my faith. Almost all of my school friends were in the service that night. If I went forward, they would know that I was a Christian. I sat frozen in place.

Should I go forward and recommit my life to Christ in front of all these people and risk losing "cool points"? Or do I stay in my seat with my Christian secret safely tucked away?

I am sure I hesitated for only a few seconds, but it felt like an eternity. Finally, I decided that, for the first time in my life, I was more concerned about what God thought of me than what people thought of me. I wanted to be a better Christian. I wanted to know God better. I no longer cared (as much) what people thought. *I knew—I love Jesus.* I got up from my seat on legs that felt like overcooked noodles and wobbled down the center aisle toward the front. With each step, I grew stronger and more confident. By the time I reached the front of the church, I was no longer aware of my friends in the pews.

As I stood up front with tears streaming down my cheeks, I asked God to forgive me for pretending not to know Him when I was around my school friends. I asked God to be more real to me than He had ever been. And I made God a promise: Never again would anyone get to know Debbye Turner without also getting to know about Jesus *in* Debbye Turner. The trajectory of my life shifted that night. I started on a new path. A path that led to the Miss America runway nine years later.

Your success hinges on faith. Not only faith in yourself but, more importantly, faith in God. It is God, and God alone, who empowers us to accomplish all the other principles of success I write about in this book.

God may tell you that what you're pursuing isn't as important as something else He has for you. He may show you something else in which your true success actually will be achieved. He may have different plans. Or perhaps His plan is for you to achieve your dream, but in a different way. God may shake up everything for you.

But I know that without God you will never be truly successful. At least, from His perspective. And His perspective matters most!

Perhaps you came to God early in life, as I did. Maybe you've strayed from Him or hidden His presence in your life, as I did as a teen. Perhaps you've never met Him at all. Whatever place you're in now, it's not too late to come to God. In faith.

THREE

Determination

Determination is essential for success. You can set what seems like an impossible goal, and then achieve it through hard work and sheer determination. Often life's *nos* are merely *not yets*.

Most people who have achieved success at some point also have faced crushing setbacks, but they determined to press ahead anyway.

I rediscovered this lesson while running my first marathon many years after being Miss America. But it was one I had learned through my pageant career.

People questioned my choice of musical instrument for the talent segment of competitions. Some felt I wasn't as pretty as other contestants. Others doubted whether I had what it took to get to the pinnacle of pageant competition—the Miss America stage.

Those questions, opinions, and doubts could not match my determination to win!

Ultimately, my setbacks could not trip me up.

Given the chance, setbacks will crush you. You must be determined not to let that happen. Do not let setbacks and related disappointment make you stumble, forsaking your dream.

Remember, you will not be the first person to experience a setback. And you won't be the last.

Do not let setbacks keep you down. Get up. Try again. And again.

Be determined not to quit until you achieve what once seemed impossible.

———

Who is a model of determination for you—a relative or friend, someone from history, someone from the Bible?

How does that person's story inspire your determination?

By refocusing from "disappointment" to "determination," how might you pivot in the midst of setback?

Despite not winning the Miss Arkansas pageant *again*, I believed that I was not supposed to give up. And my faith was strengthened by something my mother said the night I lost the Miss Arkansas pageant for the third time. Hugging me, she told me how happy she was with me. Then she whispered in my ear, "You know, there is always Missouri!"

Because I was a veterinary student in the state of Missouri, I was eligible for the Missouri preliminaries of the Miss America system. In February of 1989, I entered the Miss Columbia pageant and won. For the fourth time, I was on my way to a state pageant.

But this time, it was the Miss *Missouri* pageant.

From the moment I decided to enter the Missouri system, I no longer asked God what color dress I should wear, or what type of song I should play on the marimba, or what kind of hairstyle I should have. I only prayed, *God, lead me into Your purpose . . . just lead me into Your purpose.*

When I competed at the Miss Missouri pageant, I essentially did the very same things I had done the previous year at

Miss Arkansas. I wore the same outfits, played the very same number on the marimba—nothing different that anyone else could see.

But *I* was different—more spiritually mature and focused on God's will more than my desires.

And I was determined to try again. I didn't want my losses in the Miss Arkansas pageant to take away my dream.

I won. I became Miss Missouri 1989.

And the win qualified me to compete in the Miss America pageant.

The little girl who had never even considered the possibility that she could become Miss America was going to Atlantic City to compete on that stage. No more hiding who I really was or denying the reality of Christ's love for me. I had completely surrendered my will and desires, and with that came an overwhelming peace and assurance.

That night, on September 16, 1989, I simply wanted to be "a city on a hill"—to shine for Jesus. I was grateful and humbled, and I knew that no matter the outcome, I could trust Him. I believed with every fiber of my being that God had a plan and purpose for my life.

I believed He was going to fulfill that purpose.

I just had to be determined never to give up.

Almost from the very first time I entered a pageant—the Miss Black Teenage World pageant at fifteen years old—I was told that I could never succeed on the "big stage." In one way or another, the naysayers let me know that I didn't have the right stuff. I wasn't the right type. And there was a lot of evidence that seemed to indicate that they were right.

As a preteen, I was skinny with buck teeth and a big forehead. Kids teased me, calling me "skeleton." Some kids flicked my forehead with their thumb and forefinger because it was so prominent. Before I got braces, I was teased for having a fairly significant overbite. And when I finally had braces, I was called "metal mouth." The braces fixed my bite, and I gained some weight by the time I started competing, but I still had nothing in common with the beauty queens I saw in magazines and on television.

The first Miss America I specifically remember was Cheryl Prewitt, who won in 1979. She was a tall, leggy brunette from Mississippi. I don't actually remember the details of her stage performance, but I remember the *Jonesboro Sun* article about her the day after she won. Along with all the usual personal stats the media shares about a new Miss America, the article focused on Cheryl's claim that God healed her leg. I found her story inspiring.

As a child, Cheryl had been in a terrible car accident that badly injured her left leg, leaving it two inches shorter than the right. She walked with a limp until being prayed for at a church service. After the service, Cheryl declared boldly that God grew her leg. Her gait returned to normal. By the time she strode down the runway as the new Miss America, Cheryl walked without even a hint of a limp.

Her proclamation of being healed made newspapers around the world, including the *Jonesboro Sun*. This was the first time I'd encountered someone talking openly in a public forum like the media about God's awesome, miraculous power. Her childhood, I thought, must have been like mine. I followed Cheryl's career and ministry for many years after that. But even with her devout Christian faith, Cheryl and I were different. I did not have long, ivory, smooth legs. I did not have a flowing brown mane of hair.

And, to put it plainly, I was not White.

All the Miss Americas that I watched tearfully accept the crown, sash, and roses were White. Until 1983, when Miss New York, Vanessa Williams, captivated the judges and the entire nation. Vanessa became Miss America 1984 and the first Black Miss America to win the crown. She was a show-stopping, talented singer, whip smart, and drop-dead gorgeous. By the time Vanessa won, there had been other African American women who'd won state titles and competed on the Miss America stage, but none had broken the "rhinestone ceiling" and taken the coveted title.

Vanessa made history. And I was enthralled. Finally, a Miss America who looked like me. The African American community across the United States was over-the-moon happy for Vanessa. So many African Americans loved that she won because she was an example that beauty comes in all shades. She was an example to little Black girls that, yes, your brown skin is beautiful too.

Vanessa was a wildly popular Miss America, highly sought after to make appearances at events and perform. But ten months into her reign, nude photos of Vanessa surfaced. She ultimately relinquished the crown amidst a hurricane of outrage at the scandal.

I was eighteen at the time and had just competed in my first Miss Arkansas pageant. Not long after Vanessa's resignation, a good friend of mine told me, "Girl, you can give up this Miss America thing. After Vanessa, they won't ever let another Black girl be Miss America!" My friend was mostly being funny, but there remained the real issue of this country's long history of racial bias and oppression.

In the 1970s, a clear division existed in Jonesboro between the haves and have-nots in terms of material wealth. People faced bias due to their economic status, although the cost of people's clothing, condition of their car, or size of their house had nothing to do with the richness of their humanity. Worse? Black residents also faced discrimination.

Jim Crow laws were no longer in effect, but segregation was still rampant across the country. As in other places, Jonesboro was divided: a White side of town and a Black side of town. And yes, stereotypically, most of the Black folks lived across the railroad tracks from the White folks. My family, however, lived in a White neighborhood.

Schools were integrated by the time I came along, but at lunch and recess kids mostly retreated to their own identified racial group. There was a "Black" part of the lunchroom. The separation occurred not by force or mandate, but by choice. It was a starkly different environment than the block on which I grew up where Blacks and Whites lived side by side.

I have seen a cross burning on an African American family's front yard. I have been called the N-word many times. I have heard respectable, hardworking Black men called "boy" by White men. And at my high school, there was a yearly fight between some of the Black kids and some of the White kids. The provocation was different every year. But something would happen, or someone would say something, and a big brawl ensued.

Long before witnessing those fights, I hated the tension I felt between Black people and White people. As a young girl, I really didn't understand why people couldn't just love and respect each other. I was baffled that any human being thought they were superior to, or more valuable than, another human being.

I was surrounded by smart, compassionate, hardworking people in the African American community. How could someone not see their integrity and talents? The thought of racist people believing that my life or my mother's life or father's or any other person of color's life was in any way inferior frustrated me. I wondered: *Aren't we all God's creation? Didn't He make us all in His image?*

I don't remember integration in church on Sunday mornings

either. My experience bore out Dr. Martin Luther King Jr.'s contention that "eleven o'clock on Sunday morning is one of the most segregated hours, if not the most segregated hour, in Christian America." He uttered those words on April 17, 1960, in a *Meet the Press* interview years before I was born, and yet nothing had changed by the time my family moved to Jonesboro.

Regardless of where it reared its head, racism just made no sense to me. Even so, as a young child I bought into the fallacy of thinking that the norms of one race or culture were more desirable than others. In my case, I embraced the fallacy that "White norms are better." I thought that my bushy locks were too untamed and ugly. I wanted the long, straight, silky hair I saw on the White girls around town and in the media.

I yearned for hair like Cher's. When I was around ten years old, she and her then-husband, Sonny, were established stars. Of mixed Native American heritage, she had bone-straight, long, shiny black hair. My best friends and I wanted hair like hers. Since we didn't have it, we imagined it.

When we played house pretending to be mothers with handsome husbands and children, we pinned bath towels to our heads to emulate Cher's long, flowing hair. Thrilled with my faux mane, I would toss my head back and forth, making the towel swing through the air like Cher's hair did on TV. It was decades before I realized that my curly, fuzzy hair is perfect just how God made it.

I also secretly wanted lighter skin than my medium-brown complexion. Whites favored lighter-complexioned Blacks. But even in the African American community, certain skin tones— especially light brown, or "high yellow" as we called it—were considered more beautiful.

In the 1970s and early '80s, Black folk in my town used a popular skin-lightening cream called Ambi. Many people, including teenage me, bought it, hoping to lighten our skin to be considered more attractive. We were buying into the destructive views that made skin tone an issue and skin-lightening cream an attractive option.

These long-held views were, and continue to be, ugly vestiges of a racist, oppressive system and way of thinking. As I grew into my twenties, I finally learned that there is nothing deficient about the amount of melanin in my skin or the texture of my hair, and I began to reject such thinking. But many people still hold on to those hurtful, unfair, and inaccurate racial tropes. It breaks my heart.

———

You and I face opposition at every stage of life. Whether it is insecurity or fear or depression, we must be determined to wage spiritual battle against these life-robbing thoughts and emotions. The Bible says, "For we do not wrestle against flesh and blood, but against principalities, against powers, against the rulers of the darkness of this age, against spiritual hosts of wickedness in the heavenly places" (Ephesians 6:12 NKJV).

The implication in that verse is that we *will* wrestle. There *will be* a fight. But the key is that, as believers, we can fight differently. We don't just "put up our dukes" and hope for the best. We dress for battle. We put on and take up the whole armor of God (v. 13).

For many people, "fighting in the spirit" is like waging a bloody cage match. But according to the Bible, most of the fight is about spiritually dressing ourselves for battle. It's about getting equipped with the whole armor of God, putting on truth, righteousness, peace, faith, salvation:

> Stand therefore, having girded your waist with truth, having put on the breastplate of righteousness, and having shod your feet with the preparation of the

gospel of peace; above all, taking the shield of faith with which you will be able to quench all the fiery darts of the wicked one. And take the helmet of salvation, and the sword of the Spirit. (vv. 14–17 NKJV)

The fight is as much about shielding ourselves as it is about actual combat. Spiritual warfare is about putting on those garments that protect our mind, our soul, our life's path. Then when the onslaught comes, we use the only offensive weapon listed in Ephesians 6: the sword, which is the Word of God. So, when I face thoughts of insecurity and doubt, I fight them with the only weapon that I really have—the Word of God. When we fight with the Word of God, victory is assured.

Racism, sexism, and ageism are real, evil, and systemic. Sometimes we use those biases as an excuse to opt out, or never opt in. It's all too easy to allow these forces to be cop-outs; they become convenient excuses for quitting and not realizing our full potential.

But know this: they are nothing in the face of an all-powerful God.

God is not bound by human opposition. He is able to guide us through obstacles, over them, around them, if necessary. Because God in us is greater than the evil that is in the world (1 John 4:4).

Even though it seemed apparent that unfair bias was embedded in the systems around me, including the Miss America program, I never let prejudice or racism dictate my goals. And I was determined to fight against those voices that said I wasn't good enough.

My mother raised me to believe that I am no less or no better than any other person. So I grew up believing that I could achieve any success if I worked hard and trusted God. How life would have been different for me if my mom had not instilled that sense of worth and possibility in me!

Admittedly, people's long list of reasons that I would never win the Miss America title were hurtful, even discouraging. I was told that my boldness of faith would be an impediment. One advisor counseled me that I should "tone down the Jesus stuff." Another pageant coach lamented that while I was pretty, I was not glamorous. And countless people suggested that I change my talent away from the marimba. Time after time, I was asked if I could sing or dance or play the piano. Because, people insisted, the marimba was just too unusual.

One friend declared, "Half the people don't know what it is, and the other half don't know what to think of you playing it." But I was a good percussionist. I was determined to stick with what I knew was my strength.

———

By the time I won the Miss Missouri title, I was a junior in veterinary school. The rigor of my studies was crushing at times, but somehow I managed to keep up with my classwork and prepare to compete. Thankfully, the last two years of veterinary school at the University of Missouri–Columbia were clinical rotations, in which students rotated between different disciplines of veterinary medicine, like surgery, anesthesiology, clinical pathology, and so on.

Interspersed in those clinical rotations were "free blocks." Most students used them to get real-world experience, working alongside practicing veterinarians or conducting lab research. I arranged my schedule to have a free block during the time I competed in Miss Missouri, and spent the summer in Mexico, Missouri, where the pageant is based. That lasted until the Miss America competition, which was about two months after I won the Miss Missouri title.

This worked out well because I was able to then fully dedicate myself to preparing to compete at Miss America. Focused on competition, I spent hours each day practicing the marimba, reading newspapers, working on modeling and turning, and working out.

Exercise helped with flexibility and strength, but I struggled with weight control. After being skinny as a child, I'd blossomed into a curvy young woman. So my body did not fit the rail-thin pageant mold. I had to work consistently to keep my weight in check, but this did not come easy.

I like to eat. I never met a slice of pizza I didn't like. So preparing for the swimsuit competition was always my biggest challenge. I hated starving myself. I hated working out. I hated parading in a swimsuit on stage in high heels. But this was a part of the competition. If I wanted to win, I had to endure this awkward and sometimes cruel challenge.

I tried all sorts of tricks to beat my body into submission. I ran up flights of stairs or stadium bleachers because I'd read that doing so burned more calories than playing professional football. I wore rubber-like exercise shorts while working out because I'd read that they would make me sweat more and lose pounds. These tricks failed, and I needed to lose weight *quickly*.

The Miss Missouri committee stepped in. It hired Chuck the Butcher, a trainer famous in pageant circles because his workouts cut the fat. The problem: his regiment made me hungrier. Despite being on a restricted diet, I often snuck in a burger or a candy bar. I hid the wrappers under my car seat or in the back of a closet. Sometimes I snuck out of the house and dumped them in a stranger's garbage can blocks away. I fooled no one; the scale always gave me away.

Two weeks before I was scheduled to leave for Atlantic City to compete at Miss America, the director of the Miss Missouri pageant, Larry Webber, asked to meet with me. I was about to drive home to Arkansas to spend a little time with my mom.

I took a seat in his office and asked him what was wrong. Larry expressed concern that I hadn't lost the last ten pounds the committee felt I needed to lose in order to be ready for the swimsuit competition. I think he was afraid that I might find ten more pounds while in Arkansas with my Southern mom's awesome cooking.

"I won't beat around the bush," Larry said. "I think you could win the Miss America title. You've got what it takes." A huge smile spread across my face. It froze when he held up a hand. "But you have to be perfect in every area of competition, including swimsuit."

Tears flooded the corners of Larry's eyes. Seeing him get emotional made me emotional too. I started crying. After a few minutes, he warned, "I just don't want you to lose this opportunity because you couldn't lose a few pounds."

That stung. I was ashamed and frustrated. How maddening that all those hours—years—of practice and exercise could be washed away because my body didn't conform to an unrealistic mold. I promised Larry that I wouldn't binge on my mom's good cooking. I would lose the ten pounds, no matter what.

I tried every diet trick in the book: bananas and milk, cabbage soup, SlimFast, and grapefruit. At the time, appetite suppressants were also popular. I took those like they were candy, trying to stifle my almost constant hunger. All of these diets and tricks afforded me some success, but I just couldn't get the last few pounds off.

Then I just stopped eating altogether. Literally. I drank as much water as possible but ate no meals. I carried a candy bar in my purse, and whenever I felt faint, I'd take a single bite of it just to stay upright. It was crazy. And I don't advocate starving oneself to meet any goal or for any reason.

On those rare occasions when I couldn't resist eating, I'd immediately go to the bathroom and make myself throw it up. This was dangerous. Thankfully, repulsed by the act, I stopped. It is truly by God's grace that I didn't develop an ongoing eating disorder.

My heart goes out to those who struggle with these debilitating, life-threatening illnesses. An eating disorder is a terrible trap. From my experience, I know God's grace is available to help with battling eating disorders. My prayer is that sufferers will trust God to help them continually live free and seek help from a trained professional if needed.

Though I hit my goal weight, I was rail-thin and a dress-size two. The Miss Missouri committee and Larry were satisfied. I was famished.

I want to be clear. I was trying to fit into an unrealistic and dangerous popular notion that beauty included being extremely thin. I disagreed with it then and I disagree with it now. It is well past time to end weight-related discrimination. Women should be healthy. Period. And healthy comes in a variety of shapes and sizes.

In late August 1989, I headed to Atlantic City to compete for the Miss America crown. The contestants arrived nearly three weeks before the actual final night of competition. Activities included a week of rehearsals for the live television broadcasts, countless photo shoots, and press interviews. When the week of actual competition started, we buzzed with anticipation and excitement.

There is a slow buildup to the final night of competition that you see on television. It starts with a (then) fifteen-minute job-style interview with the judges. Each young lady stands before the panel of judges and answers all manner of questions, from our thoughts on the politics of the day, to why we deserved the win, to how to solve complex social issues. It is a rigorous process.

Seven judges seemed to simultaneously fire questions. I had to be quick, alert, and smart, yet also friendly, funny, and approachable. In the interview process, the judges were looking for a well-informed woman who was quick on her feet, able to stand up to the tough press interviews that would come as Miss America, and who was compassionate and genuinely nice. I had fifteen minutes to make my case to the judges that I could be a great Miss America. It was intense. But I loved it.

I was well prepared, thanks to my huge three-ring binder full of notes of current events and social issues. And I love a good debate, so when the tough questions and even tougher follow-ups came, I relished the opportunity to do a little intellectual sparring with the judges. The whole process was nerve-wracking for sure, but I didn't crumple under the pressure. Instead, I thrived under it. It was fun for me.

Relaxed, I demonstrated my sense of humor and wit. While swimsuit was my weakest area of competition, the interview was my strength. One former Miss Arkansas, who'd counseled me back when I was competing in the Miss Arkansas system, wisely advised me that the Miss America pageant is won or lost in the interview. I never forgot that and gave it my all during those crucial fifteen minutes.

The judges interview all fifty-one contestants, representing the fifty states and the District of Columbia. This took three days. Then the preliminary stage competition ("prelims") began. Finally, we were about to compete on the Miss America stage. The contestants are divided into three groups. Each night the groups compete in one of the competition categories: swimsuit, evening gown, and talent. During the prelims, I competed in swimsuit on the first night, talent on the second, and evening gown on the third.

I didn't quite know how I felt about taking the stage first in swimsuit. It's just strange being in a swimsuit and high heels, walking from one end of the stage to the other so the judges and audience get to see your body from all angles. By the time I was on the Miss America stage, I'd competed in swimsuit many times, so I was used to it, but I still didn't like it.

The judges in those days sought physical perfection. I'd starved myself into a canary-yellow one-piece swimsuit constructed specifically for pageant competition. Its sturdy, stretchy material sucked everything in and kept everything still. No jiggling. Yellow was a bold choice, but the color nicely matched my caramel-colored skin.

I had lots of scars (from childhood injuries and scrapes) on my legs, but I'd discovered how to cover them up using a heavy foundation created for burn victims called Dermablend. When I generously applied it to my legs, all my scars, blotches, and imperfections magically disappeared. Long before walking the Miss America stage, I had figured out how to apply the cream makeup without staining my swimsuit.

It was an elaborate process to say the least! Before the show began, I applied it to my legs, then put on three pairs of pantyhose to prevent staining. I then stepped into the swimsuit. Because it was against the rules to wear pantyhose during the swimsuit competition, I then cut them off. I developed a whole elaborate cutting pattern to remove them.

Next, I sprayed my buttocks with Firm Grip (a spray designed to help basketball players hold onto a basketball) and anchored my swimsuit in place. Couldn't have the suit riding up during the competition! As I waited backstage for my turn, I prayed a simple prayer, *God, just don't let me trip and fall. And don't let anything fall out.* When it was finally my turn, I straightened my back, pasted on my best "I got this" smile, sucked in my stomach, and sashayed on stage like I just bought the whole auditorium. I strode from backstage to center stage, making eye contact with every single judge. Then I headed downstage toward the side where the judges were seated.

When I hit my mark right in front of them, my smile got bigger. I did my turn, then looked up at the audience and headed for the opposite side of the stage. I was able to see a few people on the front couple of rows in the audience. I winked at someone just to be cute and personable. I hit my next mark, glanced back at the judges one last time, then strutted off the stage like a purebred filly.

Once I got backstage, I exhaled, released my stomach muscles and thanked God for the completion of that part of the competition. By some wondrous miracle, I won the swimsuit competition that night. I don't know if anyone else was surprised, but I sure was. That night after the show, as I drifted off to sleep, I thought, *Wow. I might have a real shot at this.* But there was no time to dwell on winning. The next prelim was coming the next night. I still had a long way to go.

Night two of the Miss America preliminary competition, I performed my talent routine. I could hardly wait. Although playing the marimba was an unusual Miss America talent, I loved it. Over the previous seven years of competing in pageants, I'd experimented with just the right marimba piece to perform onstage. I figured that even though most people were not familiar with this majestic instrument of African heritage, I should play pieces that were recognizable and enjoyable to any audience.

By the time I made it to Miss America, I'd put together a medley of three familiar tunes: "Flight of the Bumble Bee" by Nicolai Rimsky-Korsakov; "Csárdás," a Hungarian folk dance by Vittorio Monti; and the "Can-Can," the French cabaret dance by Jacques Offenbach.

I started with "Flight of the Bumble Bee" at a buzzing tempo of 220 beats per minute. Take my word for it, that's fast. Then I picked up two more mallets and performed an excerpt of "Csárdás" with the four mallets—two in each hand. Finally, I discarded the extra two mallets and finished my performance with a rousing rendition of "Can-Can." It was a fun piece that allowed me to show a lot of spunk and personality. I missed a couple of notes but tried hard not to let that show in my facial expressions. The medley usually brought the audience to their feet. The crowd cheered enthusiastically.

I'd had great success in the talent portion of the pageants in which I'd entered, but not that night. For the first time in many years, I did not win the talent preliminary award, and I was shaken. Besides the interview, talent was my strongest phase of competition. That night I went to sleep wondering what God was up to. *Did He have another first-runner-up placement in store for me?* I prayed not!

The third night of preliminary competition is a little more exciting. Front-runners emerge based on the previous nights' prelim winners, as people pick their favorites and the media speculates about the ultimate winner. The atmosphere on the Boardwalk of Atlantic City crackled with excitement. I considered it an easy night. I just had to put on my evening gown, stand up straight, and try to walk gracefully across the stage. Like the other contestants, I also had to answer a question asked by the emcee so the judges could evaluate my onstage communication skills.

That year, although we didn't know each question, we knew that it would be about our platform, an official issue or cause that each titleholder would champion during her year of service. The year I competed, "platform" was a new competition requirement. A few Miss Americas in the past had informally spoken out about a favorite cause or issue, but as of 1990, Miss America would have an official platform. Each of the state titleholders wrote an essay about three causes she felt passionate about—one of which would become her platform.

One of mine was "Motivating Youth to Excellence." I wanted young people from all stations and walks of life to know that they could achieve excellence and success with hard work and determination. So I knew that my onstage question would pertain to it. I'd studied all kinds of statistics about youth in America and was confident that I could answer any question posed to me. The night was far less hectic and nerve-wracking than the two previous nights. There is no preliminary award for evening gown, so I had no way of knowing where I ranked that evening.

I went to sleep that night thanking God for getting me so far.

And I prayed that He was not finished with me yet.

Determination is not about being encouraged and happy every day. There have certainly been days where I gave up (or thought I was giving up). There were days when I didn't see a path forward. But over the course of time, being willing to submit to the Lord and acknowledge His gentle nudging has given me the determination to press on.

You can't allow yourself to be discouraged when you have a bad day, or week, or year. At those lowest points, it's easy to give in and think you can't make it.

But we have an advocate in Jesus who ministers to and comforts us. We have the promises of God to remind us of our assured victory. Paul declares in Romans 8:28 that all things work together for our good. So what you experience now may not be good. It may feel like failure. But God promises that He will use even our failures to bring about victory.

I am a living witness that if we do not faint, but trust in the almighty, faithful God, He will bring us through. I still face times in my life that seem impossible. But because I know God is working on my behalf, I encourage myself by saying, *I don't know how this is going to work out. And I don't know when this will end. But I know God is going to sustain me. He is going to provide. He is going to bring me through.*

Because I know God is working on my behalf, I remain determined to persevere, to fight, to press on.

You can too.

FOUR

Excellence

Excellence—a lifestyle of doing and giving our very best—is a matter of choice. You must choose whether you will be defined by mediocrity or excellence.

Often it comes down to understanding the difference between what happens to us in life and what we do to make ourselves the best we can be.

You cannot always control your circumstances but you do have something to say about who and what you are when circumstances hand you an opportunity or setback.

Setbacks happen.

Focusing on goals is difficult during any crisis. But faith helps us trust God's purpose. Determination empowers us to fight doubt, fear, and indecision—and not be crushed by the weight of failure. And excellence helps us stand out from the crowd.

Excellence is not about how we feel. It's about grinding it out, doing what it takes, no matter what. Most people who live mediocre lives are living and making decisions based on how they feel. They don't feel like studying, so they don't. They don't feel like working out, so they don't. They don't feel like practicing, so they don't. And generally, their level of achievement doesn't rise above how they feel. Those who are the greatest of all time put in the work whether they felt like it or not.

That's true whether it's practicing free throws for an extra hour after team practice is over, or staying at the office to complete a report after everyone has gone home, or going to the library on Friday night when friends are at the movies, or studying for that degree when everyone else has gone to bed. Excellence is a commitment to make the necessary sacrifice that is required for success. We must learn to divorce ourselves from being ruled by comfort or convenience if we really want to achieve excellence.

> Who inspires you to pursue excellence, and why?
>
> How does knowing excellence is a *choice* provide motivation to step up your game?
>
> By refocusing from *mediocrity* to *excellence*, how might you refocus efforts to maximize your potential?

I woke up on the morning of the Miss America finals, September 16, 1989, with a strange mix of feelings. I was excited, antsy, motivated, hopeful, exhausted, and a little nervous. It had been a long eighteen days since I arrived in Atlantic City, and a long seven years since my pageant journey began.

The marathon days of rehearsals, press interviews, photo shoots, video shoots, and preliminary competitions had taken their toll. By the time the contestants reached the Miss America finals, we knew each other fairly well. We'd spent days and nights together for nearly three weeks. Like any other social situation, cliques had formed, but most of the women were nice and pleasant to be around. By the time we arrived at

Convention Hall on that Saturday morning for the final rehearsal before the live show, we joked that we were too tired to be Miss America. Whoever was left standing at the end of the night could have the crown.

I tried not to think about the crowning and made small talk with the other contestants. We talked about the foods we couldn't wait to eat when the whole ordeal was over. We talked about the boyfriends we missed or the ones we were going to dump when we got home. We speculated about what it would be like to actually be Miss America. I'd made friends with some other state titleholders who were also Christians. In the afternoon, before it was time to get dressed for the show, we stood together in a circle, held hands, and prayed.

I don't know what words I prayed aloud, but silently I thanked God for getting me that far. It had been a long, difficult road filled with ups and downs, setbacks and disappointments. My mother scrimped and scraped to raise money to finance my participation. I thanked God for the wins and losses, for all those first-runner-up placements, for the scores of people who encouraged and supported and believed in me. And although I wasn't representing the state in which I'd grown up, I thanked God that I was there representing Missouri, the "Show Me" state. And boy, had Missouri ever shown me love and support.

The Miss Missouri pageant board generously provided everything I needed to compete well at Miss America. I finally had a designer evening gown, custom-designed just for me by Stephen Yearick. I had a fire-engine red, beaded pantsuit for my talent competition. And this time I didn't have to bead the fabric myself. The Miss Missouri folks even made sure I had decent undergarments and hosiery. God had placed me in the right place, with the right people who spared no expense to enhance my chances of success. I was grateful beyond words.

Achieving a goal is rarely a solo act. We need the support of others who provide needed resources, just in the knick of time!

As the group prayer ended, we all dispersed to our designated spots in the dressing room to put on makeup and style our hair. As I applied my makeup and put curlers in my hair, I prayed one last prayer.

God, I did everything I knew to do to get ready for this moment. I practiced, and studied, and rehearsed, and took advice, and fasted and prayed. I did everything I could possibly do. Now I need You to do what only You can do. If it is Your will for me to be Miss America at the end of this evening, touch the hearts of the judges. Help me to perform excellently tonight. I am in Your hands.

Prayer complete, I felt at peace. I had no guarantees that I would win. All I could do was give it my all and trust God to do the rest.

The day of the Miss America finals was surreal. We arrived early in the morning with everything we needed to compete because we would be locked into Convention Hall, the location of the pageant, and couldn't leave until after the show ended around midnight. We sat around—a lot—while the television crew set lighting and determined camera angles. We repeatedly rehearsed the choreographed production numbers. We rehearsed what do to if we were named in the top ten semifinalists. And we rehearsed what to do if we won the crown.

The final night of competition is a blur to me now. I remember snippets of specific moments. I remember being in my spot for the opening of the show. In those days, the Miss America telecast included elaborate production numbers and the opening production was designed to kick things off with a bang. We were separated into different groups that would enter the stage from several angles, stage left, stage right, and from the far end of the runway. I was in the group that started at the far end of the runway. My group was escorted by security officers through the audience, then directed to take our places.

The Miss America runway is iconic. It was nearly a full city block long. And by the end of the evening one of us would walk down that runway with the crown on her head.

When showtime finally arrived, I was so excited I could barely stand still. My fellow contestants and I wished each other well, high-fived, fist-bumped, and hugged. Finally, the music started and a booming voice declared, "Live! From the Convention Hall in Atlantic City, New Jersey . . . the Miss America pageant!"

That was our cue. The live show began. Our production music started. We gave each other last-minute hugs. Off we went up the runway toward the stage, singing at the top of our voice, "I can fly! I can go forever. I run and jump and break away. . . ." My face could barely hold my smile. I'd never felt like that before. Exhilaration, humility, and awe. Here I was, a little Black girl from Jonesboro, Arkansas, raised in a single parent, lower-middle-class home, on national television as a contestant in the Miss America pageant.

In 1989, the Miss America telecast was the second-highest-viewed live television program of the year, just behind the Super Bowl. Thirty-five million people tuned in from around the world. And there were twenty thousand people in the live audience. The crowd's roar was deafening. I could barely hear the music. But I didn't care. I'd made it. I was competing for Miss America. *Thank you, Jesus!*

After the opening production number, Gary Collins and Miss America 1971, Phyllis George—the emcees for the show—would announce the ten contestants who had scored the highest during the preliminary competition. This information had been a closely guarded secret. No one other than the judges and auditors knew who had made the ten semifinal slots until it was announced live on the air. Those ten ladies would then compete in all three areas of stage competition on live television for the title Miss America 1990.

The names were being called and, just like at the state pageants, I whispered a prayer. There was no way I could win Miss America if I didn't make the top ten. And then I heard it. My name was the ninth to be called. That was it! I'd made top ten. I had no time to celebrate or revel, though.

The night went by in a flurry of lightning-fast costume changes, and blink-and-you'll-miss-it stage performances. I had no time to be nervous. I had no time to reflect on what this all meant. I had to be in the right outfit at the right time, hit my mark, and do my very best. I have absolutely no memory of the swimsuit competition. I suspect I blocked the whole humiliating experience out of my memory. Then it was time to play my marimba.

This competition was a little slower. Each contestant was allotted one minute fifty seconds for her talent routine. Since I was the ninth in the order, I changed out of my swimsuit and into my talent costume with time to spare. As I sat backstage, I ran through my piece in my head, visualizing the tricky parts and what I needed to do to navigate them accurately. Because I started with "Flight of the Bumble Bee" at 220 beats per minute, I stretched my hands and arms so they would be loose and ready to fly across the marimba keys.

During the commercial break, before my talent segment, a member of the stage crew came up to me and started making small talk. I'm a focused person, especially in stressful times, so I was in no mood for chitchat, but I also welcomed the distraction. I couldn't play accurately if my hands were trembling from nervousness.

He asked me where I was from and a few similar questions. Somehow we started talking about music and I told him that I knew a Christian rap, a hip-hop song. He convinced me to rap a little for him. The show was still in commercial, so I thought *why not.*

"My name is Debbye Turner and I'm hot as a burner and I rap to a T. So everybody that's sittin' around, stop and listen . . . to me." I rapped a few more lines and then I was called to take my place on stage. The commercial break was ending. I hurried to my marimba, center stage, stretched my hands one last time, and waited for Gary Collins to introduce me. I gave the conversation I had backstage with the stage crew member no more thought. It was time to play my heart out. But that conversation would later play a significant role in my year as Miss America.

Gary finished my introduction, my accompaniment music began, and away I went. I missed a couple of notes, but I was happy with my performance overall. Again, I had no time to celebrate; I had to change into my evening gown.

When you watch the Miss America pageant, you see these beautiful, graceful, composed young women on stage. But the second we get backstage, we take off running to get ready for the next phase of competition. At times, we have only seconds to completely change and be back on stage, trying our best to look graceful and composed once again.

Each contestant has a hostess assigned to her, someone to help with the changes and any quick fixes—a broken zipper, a popped button, an accidental stain. These women are angels. They zip up dresses, tuck in what needs to be tucked in, arrange out-of-place strands of hair, and dry anxiety-induced tears before they ruin our makeup. We couldn't make it back out on stage so quickly without them.

I was ready just in time for the evening gown competition. First, I needed to float across the stage like a queen, execute my turns like a supermodel, and then stop at the microphone set up in the middle of the stage to answer a question about youth motivation, my potential official platform as Miss America.

My onstage question went something like, "Considering all of the challenges facing today's youth, how do you plan to motivate youth to excellence?"

I had practiced answering that question countless times. I was ready, or so I thought.

The funny thing is, when you are on live TV, in front of millions of people, the mind can betray you. Combine that with the fact that we only had fifteen seconds to answer. Fifteen seconds to sound intelligent, thoughtful, inspirational, and passionate. It's a tall order. And that was my final opportunity to compete in front of the judges. The last chance to impress them. The last chance to convince them that I was the right choice. That was the first time all evening I felt pressure.

Honestly, I didn't like my answer. I could see the timer counting down. That messed with my head. I blurted out something about telling kids that they can do anything they dream about and then show them the way to do it. Honestly, it wasn't my finest moment.

After the top ten contestants had competed, the judges submitted their final scores. And we waited. There was a long commercial break to give the auditors time to tally all the scores. I was numb. I was even out of prayers. It had all been done. It was out of my hands.

During the final seconds of the last commercial break, the stage crew placed the top ten semifinalists on stage in preparation for the announcement of the finalists and the winner. It was impossible to think over the cacophony in Convention Hall. Delegations from each state hooted and hollered for their state titleholder. Some people chanted the name of the state that they wanted to win. Gary Collins and Phyllis George made small talk at the microphone, trying to fill time while the results were tabulated.

My head was swimming. I couldn't even remember what I'd just done during the competition. I was hungry and my feet hurt. I was ready for the winner to be announced, if for no other reason than to take off my high heels! Finally, we were back on air. It was time to find out who would be crowned Miss America.

Gary and Phyllis started with the fourth runner-up. Just like in Arkansas and Missouri, I prayed silently, *Lord, your will be done.* It was Miss Ohio. Then the third runner-up. *Lord, your will be done.* It was Miss Illinois. Then Gary Collins got to the second runner-up and when he announced the name, my heart almost stopped. He proclaimed, "The second runner-up and the winner of a fourteen thousand dollar scholarship is Debbie—"

Oh no. Oh no. Oh no.

"Riecks."

Debbie Riecks was Miss Colorado and placed second runner-up. That left six of us standing on stage.

Gary and Phyllis then told the audience that they were about to call out two names. One would be the first runner-up and the other would be the new Miss America. "Virginia Cha, Miss Maryland, and Debbye Turner, Miss Missouri."

The excitement in Convention Hall reached a fever pitch. Virginia's supporters began screaming support for her. And those supporting me were cheering just as loud. While most of the night up to this point is a blur, I remember in fine detail what happened next. I left the line of the remaining five top ten semifinalists and joined Virginia at center stage. I hugged her and congratulated her on her momentous accomplishment. To get this far, even without actually winning, was a big deal.

Virginia looked like she wanted to faint. Her chest was heaving up and down. After our hug, we held hands (like pageant finalists often do) and waited to hear the final result. As Gary went on and on about how exciting this moment was and how one of our lives was going to change forever, I thought Virginia was going to hyperventilate. To relieve some of the tension of the moment, I began to talk to her. I told her she'd done a great job. I said, "Oh my, can you believe we're here?" Gary Collins kept babbling to stretch out the moment and build excitement.

Finally, Phyllis admonished Gary to hurry up and announce the winner. I heard Phyllis say this and looked her direction and nodded in agreement. With nothing left to say, Gary finally said, "Ladies and Gentlemen, the winner of a twenty thousand dollar scholarship . . . and our first runner-up is . . . Virginia Cha, Miss Maryland!"

I closed my eyes for a brief moment. I was relieved that Gary had not called my name. The music for that iconic serenade "There She Is" began to swell. I turned to hug Virginia as she turned to hug me. I was really just congratulating her for her great achievement. She had performed beautifully. She was an impeccable classical pianist, gorgeous, super smart, and very deserving. I truly commended her for a job well done.

In the middle of this very polite, congratulatory hug, it hit me. I won!

Virginia was first runner-up; *I* was Miss America. My polite hug turned into a bear hug. I trembled with excitement. I laughed uncontrollably. Elation doesn't begin to describe the feeling. I released Virginia and my hands shot straight up in the air toward heaven. I lifted my face upward and said, out loud, "Thank You!"

Yes, my first action as Miss America was to acknowledge and thank my almighty, good God. I looked toward the judges seated in front of the stage and thanked them. I was handed the Miss America scepter. I grabbed it with both hands. Then I gave a thumbs-up. I pumped that thumb up and down several times. I wanted to make sure my mother saw me doing it. That was our special signal. Each time I won a pageant, I did the same, acknowledging that I couldn't have done it without her. My mother's love, support, sacrifice, and prayers had propelled me to this point. I couldn't see my mom from the stage, but I wanted her to know that she was in my thoughts at that moment.

Then Gretchen Carlson, Miss America 1989, approached me with my new crown. There is quite a difference between Gretchen's height and mine, so I had to bend my knees so she could reach the top of my head and pin on the crown. I could barely stay still while she anchored that symbol of achievement onto my heavily sprayed hair. I kept bouncing up and down with excitement. Poor Gretchen tried her best to finish her last duty as the outgoing Miss America. She finally got the crown pinned down.

"Congratulations. You're Miss America," she whispered, bracing my shoulders in both hands.

"Miss America, the runway is yours," Gary Collins said.

I mouthed a thank-you to him (I would have thanked anybody for anything in that moment) and headed down the runway. The orchestra played. People were on their feet, clapping and cheering. I wanted to cry but for some odd reason I couldn't.

The emotion of the moment was so heavy it felt like a thick wool blanket enveloping me, but I couldn't cry. I guess I had already done all my crying in the years leading up to this moment. I'd cried when people's harsh words hurt my feelings. I'd cried when I thought I was going to win a pageant and I didn't. Maybe I was all cried out.

All I could do was smile a grin too big for my face. Truthfully, I was a little frustrated with it. Just like for the marimba, the interview, the walking on stage, I had practiced my winning smile in the weeks leading up to Miss America. I knew that if I won, those initial photos of my reaction to winning would last forever. I wanted to look good. I know that's vain, but it's the truth. I was so overcome with emotion that I couldn't control my facial muscles. It wasn't the smile I had practiced, and I was powerless to change it. A couple of times, I relaxed my face and stopped smiling altogether to try to reset. That didn't work. Every time I smiled, it was a big, goofy thing.

Besides the battle with my facial muscles, an avalanche of thoughts and emotions overwhelmed me. As I took that storied walk down that storied runway, waving, flashing thumbs-up, flashbacks were playing in my head. I thought about those early days in pageants when my mom made my costumes on her Singer sewing machine at our dining room table.

I thought about the hundreds of times I strolled back and forth in our unfinished basement in front of a full-length mirror. I remembered the times that Jonesboro High School and Arkansas State University loaned me their marimbas because I didn't own one, and the thousands of hours of practice; missing parties, movies, and hanging out with friends.

I thought of the countless times that I disassembled the marimba and crammed it into my Nissan Sentra in order to get to a pageant location. I thought about the times my mom and her friends laid hands on me and prayed for me before pageant competitions, and the times I cried because I didn't win. I reflected on all the people who said this moment would never—could never—happen. And I recalled the people who encouraged me to keep trying.

I thought about a boy I had a crush on in middle school, who didn't return my crush. He once cruelly said to me that I would be halfway cute if I would get some braces and do something about my crooked teeth. As I strode down the runway in Atlantic City's Convention Hall, I thought that if I could see that young man again, I would ask him, "How do you like me now?"

I finally made it to the end of the runway. My family and friends were seated deep in the audience. At the end of the runway, I could see them cheering and jumping and crying. I threw my thumb in the air one more time. I wanted my mom to know that she deserved that moment too.

It was all for naught, though. My mom and the rest of my family were so busy celebrating with each other, nobody was looking my way. They were back-slapping and high-fiving each other. I stood there a moment hoping to catch their attention. Nope.

So, I looked straight into the camera, waved, and mouthed "Hi, Columbia"—my shout-out to Columbia, Missouri. The local pageant that took me to Miss Missouri was Miss Columbia. And it was where I'd lived for the previous three years while in veterinary school. I looked my mom's way one more time. She was surrounded by people hugging and congratulating her.

Oh well. She'll see it on the videotape, I thought.

The stage director signaled for me to head back to the main stage. The show was about to end. I turned to walk back the way I'd come. On the way back to center stage, I caught a glimpse of myself on the Jumbotron, the giant screen that showed what was being telecast around the world.

"There she is. Walking on air she is. Fairest of the fair she is . . . Miiiissssss Aaaammmmmeriiiiicaaaaa," and "There She Is" came to its renowned dramatic end.

As I reached the main stage, the other contestants rushed toward me like water breaking through a dam. We hugged and kissed and giggled. So many of the contestants whom I'd gotten to know over those last three weeks seemed genuinely happy for me. This was an end to a long, difficult journey for all of us.

For me, Miss America, it was also the beginning of another journey that would prove to be even harder than what I'd just come through.

———

That night, September 16, 1989, was a glorious night. I'll never forget it.

But it's important to put success into perspective.

Miss America didn't make me excellent. I was the same Debbye before that evening as I was after the crown was put on my head. Certainly, the excellence I had pursued in my life, the measure of excellence that God had helped me achieve within, was helpful in the competition. But at the same time, I wasn't in control of the circumstance that put that crown on my head. I wasn't a better Debbye because I'd won.

This is so important for us all to realize, for you to understand. You pursue excellence not because it is a guarantee of a new career or a better house or winning an honor like Miss America. You pursue excellence because an excellent God created you for excellence. It is your birthright.

Sometimes the spotlight will shine on you, and people may applaud you for some excellent thing you've achieved. But know that the circumstance comes from God.

Your real reward is in the light of His pleasure.

FIVE

Authenticity

One of the popular phrases of the early twenty-first century is "You do you, Boo." In other words, be yourself. Don't let anyone or anything define who you are and what you do.

Through my years of pageant competition, advisors, counselors, and trainers would give me a laundry list of ways I needed to improve or change in order to be successful in the Miss America system. They'd usually end with, "Just be yourself." I always thought that was funny. *Tell me to stand up ramrod straight, with my hips pushed slightly forward, stomach sucked in, rib cage pushed out, head tilted ever so subtly, shoulders back, chin up, eyes wide, smile big-but-not-too-big, hands loosely at my side, feet in the "model T" position . . . and act natural. Be yourself. Ha!* That seemed ludicrous.

But the concept of "being yourself" is far from ridiculous. Authenticity is a key element to success. You were created to be uniquely you. And any effort to conform to a mold, copy another person, or change with the shifting tide only diminishes the single most powerful advantage you have in life. Being *you*. There is not another one of you on the earth. There never has been nor will there ever be. No one can be you like you can. That's an amazing advantage. Don't squander it.

Being your true self is your true path to success. There are people who live their whole lives competing with others, trying to fit into some "norm," or living up to someone else's expectation—and never really discover who they were created to be. That is a real tragedy.

One of our most important accomplishments in life is to embark on this journey of self-discovery. Who are you *really*? What are your passions? What makes you righteously angry? What keeps you awake at night? What gets you out of bed in the morning? What fills you with unexplainable joy? The answers to these questions are clues to your authentic self.

Don't let stereotypical expectations, peer pressure, or conventional wisdom dictate your identity. God made us uniquely different for a reason. He wants you to bring something to the table that can only come from you. The vast diversity of this earth is the core of its exquisite beauty. That applies to you as well.

Resist popular belief. Resist unreasonable expectations. Resist the urge to conform in order to fit in. There is a place for you that is designed specifically for you. Being anything other than your authentic self means you can't fit into that place. And you miss the real success that comes from authenticity. Don't get me wrong, you can be "successful" while being inauthentic, but it won't be fulfilling. It won't feel right.

The greatest success that you can achieve is to be exactly who God created you to be. That's true authenticity.

———

The second the music stopped, the camera lights dimmed, and the telecast of the Miss America pageant ended, my life as Miss America began.

It was a little past midnight. Leonard Horn, then chief

executive officer of the Miss America Organization, introduced himself to me. I was still on the stage, surrounded by the other contestants, barely able to breathe from the excitement of winning. As Convention Hall's house lights came up, Leonard began ushering me toward a room off the backstage area, designated for a press conference. As he led me to the Press Galley, he prepared me for what was about to occur.

"You are about to face media from around the world as Miss America for the first time," he said. "They will ask you all sorts of questions. You can answer the questions any way you want. You can answer any questions that you want to answer. The Miss America Organization does not tell you what to say or what not to say. But be careful, what you say can and will be held against you."

I think I laughed a little at that odd pep talk. Leonard did not crack a smile. I would soon learn why he was so serious.

We entered the Press Galley and someone introduced the new Miss America 1990.

Oh wow, that's me! I thought.

I stepped up to the podium and expressed my elation and gratitude for the immense honor of becoming Miss America 1990. I spoke briefly about my childhood and journey in pageants that led to my victory. Then came the reporters' questions.

"Describe how you feel in this moment," a reporter asked.

That first question was easy to answer. I expected it. The next question was predictable as well.

"What were you thinking as you walked down the runway as the new Miss America?"

I joked that I was thinking about taking off my high heels and eating pepperoni pizza—because my feet hurt and I was starving. The room full of journalists from around the world roared with laughter. I relaxed a bit, confident that I could handle my first press conference with ease.

As I exhaled the first unexpected curveball was thrown.

"How do you feel being a role model for little Black girls around the country?"

The question surprised and offended me. I was surprised because I naively thought that the color of my skin had nothing to do with anything. And I was offended because I wasn't Miss Black America. I was Miss America. I answered that I hoped that I could be an inspiration to *all* little girls, and little boys too. I went on to say that being Black is just a part of who I am.

"I am a born-again Christian, a veterinary student, a musician, and animal lover," I continued. "There are many facets to my identity. Being Black is just one of them."

There! I taught that narrow-minded reporter a lesson.

I was proud of my answer. Little did I know that I would learn a critical lesson the next day because of that reporter.

After the press conference, there were a seemingly endless series of receptions and parties at which I made appearances, much like all the Inaugural Balls held when the President of the United States takes office. At each party, I made a short speech, took pictures with key people like pageant officials and corporate sponsors, and then was whisked away to the next soiree.

At some point, there was an official photo shoot with me in my new Miss America crown and shots of me with my family. This was the first time I'd seen them since the crowning. My mom, dad, and sister beamed with joy. My mom had that "I knew this was going to happen" look on her face. We hugged a long time.

Finally, around 3:00 a.m., I was finished with the parties, pictures, and speeches. When I arrived at my hotel, to my delight, I learned that I had been upgraded to a new room, a luxury suite. I'd never seen such opulence. The floors were marble. There were marble columns everywhere. The suite was nearly as large as the house I grew up in, with a living room, dining room, giant bedroom, marble-covered bathroom, and a spectacular view of the Atlantic City boardwalk and the Atlantic Ocean. To top it off, there was a giant Jacuzzi . . . in the living room!

My family and close friends were allowed to come to my new suite for a short celebration. We laughed and high-fived and hugged some more. I think the sentiment among us was, "Can you believe this actually happened?" I didn't have long with my family and friends. By this time, it was nearly 4:00 a.m. Everyone was ushered out of the room so I could get some sleep before a big day of firsts as Miss America. I was so giddy, though, that there was no chance of me going to sleep quickly.

Once everyone left, I was in the suite with one of the two traveling companions who would be with me throughout the coming year. We'd met a couple of hours earlier. She offered to unzip the white-velvet, silk, and rhinestone evening gown I still wore. I told her that I was hungry and wanted to try out the snazzy Jacuzzi. We ordered pizza. I put on my swimsuit and then sat in the Jacuzzi, eating. Other than the moment I won the pageant, this was the best moment of my life.

Exhausted, I finally laid across the bed around 6:00 a.m., about an hour before my first duty as Miss America. I drifted off to sleep for a few minutes with the crown in my hands. Forty-five minutes later, I was up, dressed, and headed for the photo shoot every new Miss America takes on the Atlantic City beach.

The most iconic photo was always of the newly crowned winner in shorts and a T-shirt frolicking in the surf of the Atlantic Ocean. I had seen many of these shots of previous Miss Americas over the years, so I expected this. But I was worried. While my hair was straightened with a relaxer that calmed the natural curls and frizz of my hair, it was no match for the humidity of a September morning at the ocean.

Time was not on my hair's side. If I stayed on the beach too long my hair would swell into a big frizzy puff, which is not the look I was going for in that moment.

I tried to smile just right, tilt my head, and position my arms exactly as the photographer instructed, to speed up the shoot. Of course, it took a while, plus there were several members of the media also trying to photograph me.

After a quick change into a more formal outfit and a re-styling of my hair, I was off to more press interviews, posing for pictures, and a brunch in my honor.

Many of the pageant volunteers from around the country attended. My family was there as well. This was the last time I would see them for quite some time. I was about to travel the country as Miss America. For the next year, I would live out of two large suitcases, going from city to city, hotel room to hotel room.

I'd only been Miss America for twelve hours but already I felt the seismic shift that had occurred. In that short time, I was no longer *just* the baby daughter of Gussie and Fred, younger sister of Suzette, veterinary student, and little Black girl from Arkansas.

I was Miss America.

That auspicious title came with a whole new set of people's preconceived notions and huge expectations. There was no gradual buildup. I slammed full speed into a wall called "being Miss America." Suddenly, people were doing things for me: packing my luggage, planning my schedule, making decisions on my behalf. My head spun. I went into survival mode because of the deluge of activities and responsibilities. I had no hope of keeping up with all the duties and related details on my own. I needed to ask my traveling companion, "OK, what's next?"

It's hard to describe life as Miss America. Nothing in normal life compares to that schedule. It's similar to what I would imagine running for president of the United States must be: a whirlwind experience from day one! I traveled twenty thousand miles a month. I was in a different city every eighteen to thirty-six hours. Once, I was in five states in a single day! I worked seven days a week for forty-eight weeks of that year. I gave several speeches a day, to different groups. I signed countless autographs and posed for endless photos.

I'll always remember the night that I won the pageant and answered that reporter's fateful question: "How do you feel being a role model for little Black girls around the country?" During my response, I explained how my skin color was just a part of my identity. To my horror, the quote in many newspapers the next morning was "Being Black is the least of who I am." That was not at all what I meant to say. Yet I would spend the rest of the year clarifying it.

As you might imagine, some in the African American community were alarmed that I seemed to hold no pride in my ethnicity. Nothing was further from the truth. Yet I was criticized for disavowing my race. I hadn't done that, but the damage was done. For months I was asked to explain what I meant and defend why I was ashamed of my skin color. It was maddening.

I learned quickly that I had to be intentional about *what* I said and *how* I said it. I learned that word choice matters a great deal. I had to say what I meant and mean what I said. I tried very hard to never make that mistake again.

It felt like there was a bright spotlight on me at all times. It seemed as if people were waiting for me to make a wrong move or say the wrong thing (again), and then pounce.

I learned many years later that the Miss America officials held their collective breath my entire year, wondering if some scandal was going to emerge. I was the second African American ever to win the title, and the third African American to be Miss America. After Vanessa Williams resigned in 1984, the first runner-up, Suzette Charles, also African American, assumed the title. Many wondered if there was some skeleton in my closet that would tumble out during my year.

The hopes of the African American community to see me succeed enveloped and smothered me at the same time. I was analyzed and criticized about whether I was "black enough." Yet I felt I needed to represent everyone, as all Miss Americas are supposed to do, so I didn't want to be seen as "the *Black* Miss America." Don't get me wrong. I was—and still am—proud of my heritage and ancestry. And I was tickled when the African American community embraced me.

One of my first appearances after winning Miss America was at the King of Prussia Mall near Philadelphia. It was an autograph session and the line of people waiting to meet me stretched almost the entire mall. I sat for hours signing autographs and greeting people. Toward the end of the session, an elderly African American woman was next in line. She was very thin, slightly bent, with smooth brown skin and bright, twinkly eyes. When it was her turn for an autograph, she grabbed my hands and told me how proud she was that I won. She noted that she had traveled two hours and stood in line for hours to meet me. I was deeply honored.

"And you know what I like best about you?" she asked, looking directly into my eyes.

"No ma'am. What is that?"

She let go of one of my hands, gently pinched my cheek and declared, "You *look* Black!"

"Yes, ma'am, I sure do. Thank you." I blurted between chuckles. I thought I would fall off my chair laughing.

It was in that moment I realized I had a responsibility I hadn't had before.

When that woman uttered the words, "You look Black!" it carried an unspoken message: It was important to her that I represent my ancestry well and with pride. Suddenly, I understood better why so many had objected to my feeble attempt at being colorless. I hadn't stepped up to take on my responsibility to others. Trying to ignore, or diminish, my color was tantamount to denying how God made me. God made me brown. And that's a good thing. Skin color does not determine our value or abilities. But it does tell of our history and heritage. I would never dismiss my culture again.

Being my authentic self, an African American woman with brown skin, sometimes frizzy hair, and unapologetically Christian were things to embrace, not bury or minimize. When we are authentic in who we are and how we live, it gives others around us permission to be their authentic selves. Authenticity is contagious.

Beyond the reporter's role model question, the first two weeks of being Miss America were like some weird, sequin-coated initiation. Every waking minute was filled with activity. I made appearances on the most-watched shows at the time, including the *Today Show*, *Live with Regis and Kathie Lee*, *David Letterman Show*, *Home Show*, and the *700 Club* on the Trinity Broadcasting Network. When I wasn't making a television appearance, I was doing a radio, magazine, or newspaper interview. I also made appearances at events held by the Miss America corporate sponsors.

I'll never forget my experience selecting some of my Miss America outfits. In those days, one of the sponsors was the Crafted with Pride in U.S.A. Council, a trade organization that promoted apparel manufactured in America. It donated a complete wardrobe to Miss America. A couple days after winning the title, I walked into a hotel ballroom filled with racks of clothing to select whatever I liked. I needed numerous outfits for all the appearances that I'd make as Miss America. Most of the collections were available in Sears, JC Penney, and Wal-Mart. I was grateful for them and wore them with pride. The experience was mind-blowing.

I'd grown up lower-middle class. My mom made many of my clothes on her Singer sewing machine when I was a little girl. And when I got older, my clothes were those she bought for me on sale or from a discount store. So this was an exotic new experience. We just couldn't afford high-priced, designer clothes.

There was a time when my mother owned only two dresses—both of which she'd made. She would hand-wash the one she wasn't wearing and hang it on the clothesline in our backyard to dry so it would be clean and fresh for the next day. I never heard my mom complain about her meager wardrobe. She did what she had to do. During that same time, she made sure that I had what I needed for school—a new lunch box each year, properly fitting shoes, and other supplies. I didn't notice her sacrifice then. I also never stopped to wonder why she didn't wear a winter coat. I just figured she wasn't that cold. But I came to understand as I matured and became more aware of the world around me that she would forgo a coat for herself to make sure that my sister and I had coats.

I would have happily taken all the outfits in that hotel ballroom, except I was limited to what could fit into my two large traveling suitcases.

Being Miss America struck at the core of my identity—in other people's eyes. In the space of a few hours, very few people viewed me as "just Debbye." As my reign continued, people wanted to know about Miss America. It was hard to process how people treated me differently. Even some of my friends treated me differently. I called one of my close college friends just a few days after winning the title. I was a little homesick and just wanted to hear a familiar voice. When she answered the phone and realized it was me calling, her response was, "Oh my, Miss America is calling me!"

I know she meant no harm by her effusive reaction, but her comment broke my heart. In that moment, I didn't want to be Miss America. I wanted to be Debbye talking to one of my dear friends. She was so excited that I'd won. And she wanted to hear all the juicy details about my experience. I understood, but it was disheartening. I knew during that conversation that my life would never be the same. I knew then that many people would see the title first and foremost.

I was right.

The most repeated phrase that I used during those early months as Miss America was, "I'm still just Debbye." I did so because everywhere I went people recognized me as the new Miss America. Most wanted my autograph, or a picture taken with me.

I'll never forget one encounter in a public restroom. I was in a stall when I heard a group of noisy, giggly girls come in. I thought nothing of it until I overheard one of them whisper, "Miss America is in here." Another replied, "Oh yeah? Where?" One responded, "Those are her feet right there!"

I was more than a little embarrassed, but eventually I had to emerge from the stall. They gawked as I made my way to the sink to wash my hands. I smiled at them and said, "Yes, it's me." They screamed in delight. I guess they'd never seen a Miss America close up, or in a public bathroom. That encounter reminded me how differently people view "celebrities."

People's response to me as Miss America changed my social calculus. I began wondering what people wanted from me. Did people like me because of the crown, or did they really like *me*? I could never be sure of their motives. That uncertainty set into motion an anxiety that would later blossom into full-blown depression.

There were awesome perks to being Miss America. But at the end of the day, in my hotel room, when all the clamor and activity was over, I was desperately lonely. I couldn't sit on the couch and talk through my day with my mom or drop by a friend's house to gab about my innermost thoughts.

Complicating my loneliness during my reign as Miss America was the fact that I was Miss America before cell phones, FaceTime, social media, and all the technological advances we enjoy today. My family didn't know how to reach me unless I called them from my hotel room and gave them the number, which changed almost daily due to my intense travel schedule.

Although I was lonely, I was not alone on the road. I traveled with two wonderful women, Ellie Ross and Bonnie Sirgany. They alternated months being on the road with me. Ellie had traveled with many Miss Americas before me and was an old pro. I jokingly called her "the real queen." She knew all the complexities of the Miss America experience. She gave me sound advice, knew before I did when I was about to have a meltdown, and comforted me with her wicked sense of humor. She became a surrogate mom to me during that year. Bonnie was new on the job. She was a bit younger than Ellie and more like a cool aunt. She was organized, sometimes better dressed than I was, and fiercely protective.

These fabulous ladies were lifesavers. They managed my day-to-day schedule, making sure I was ready on time, including at the airport for flights. They fulfilled adoring fans' requests to take pictures of me. They also met smaller needs, like providing a tissue, breath mint, or safety pin at the opportune time. They carried my purse more than I did. No matter where I went, they were always nearby, right in the background waiting to give me what I needed, or to protect me from anyone who tried to get too close.

Every day was different, but there were some constants. Most days included at least one autograph session. I would sit at a table in a drugstore or mall with a sign that said, "Meet Miss America 1990." Sometimes there were lines that snaked out of the store and down the block. I would shake hands, make brief small talk, and sign autographs on my official Miss America headshots for hours on end—some days my right hand cramped from holding a pen and writing my name. Most days also included several speeches. I addressed local business organizations, corporations, women's groups, local and state legislators, and lots of young people.

Being Miss America was exhausting, but a blast. I met many celebrities and politicians. I met with President George H. W. Bush in the Oval Office. I attended tapings of popular shows, including *Saturday Night Live* and *The Cosby Show*. I got the great table at the hottest restaurants. I flew first-class and rode in stretch limousines, often with a police escort. I got front-row seats at Broadway shows.

Oprah Winfrey invited me and my mom to be on her talk show for an episode about celebrities and their moms. The show gave the mothers makeovers. My mom and Oprah connected in a special way. And Mommy loved being featured on the show. You would have thought *she* was Miss America.

The night before the show's taping was eventful. Oprah had invited me, my sister, and my mom to have dinner with her! Oprah was dealing with a stalker at the time, and she showed up at the restaurant where we'd just eaten. We'd had a lovely time and were crossing the sidewalk from the restaurant to the car when she approached Oprah. We all quickly got in the car and drove away, but the encounter unnerved Oprah.

My mom offered to pray for Oprah, and she accepted my mother's offer. So, in the back of a stretch limousine, we held hands and prayed. At first I was a bit embarrassed by my mother's request to pray. This. Was. Oprah. Winfrey. But I was reminded that night that we should be a witness for Christ everywhere we go. And we should share God's love with everyone we meet, no matter who they are. Oprah thanked my mom for her prayer. Silently, I thanked God for my mother.

Like Oprah, I also dealt with unnerving situations. Along with all the attention of being Miss America came that less savory aspect of being famous: stalkers and death threats. I had my share of both. I also received hundreds of letters from inmates who declared their love for me and promised to find me when released. And not everyone was happy that Miss America was African American. I got nasty mail from some narrow-minded, hateful people that was downright alarming.

One death threat was credible enough that the FBI got involved. An appearance in Georgia was canceled because local law enforcement couldn't guarantee my safety. I had to stay in my hotel room with the curtains drawn and a police officer stationed outside my door. I prayed that God would place an angel right next to him, in case he needed backup. I don't remember if they found the person who made the threat. But I went to the next city on my schedule and prayed that God would protect me from all danger, seen and unseen. And He did.

Another reality that came with fame was sensational, often untrue, "news" coverage. I became fodder for tabloid papers and television shows. Not long after I won Miss America, a picture of me in the yellow swimsuit I'd worn during the pageant appeared on the cover of the *National Enquirer*. The headline read something like, "Miss America Vows to Never Get Married." The accompanying article stated that because of my religion I would never marry. There were "quotes" from people, including my mother. None of it was true. Not one word.

My mom had never spoken to the *National Enquirer*. And I don't know the identity of the so-called "friend" quoted in the article. The write-up went on to declare that Mike Tyson wanted to date me and had sent me flowers to try to woo me. Absolutely untrue. I'd never received any flowers from the boxing heavyweight champ. And, for that matter, I'd never even met him.

I was distraught when the article was published. How could they just make stuff up like that and get away with it? I complained to my mom about it one day, hoping for some sympathy. She just laughed and said, "Sweetheart, you've made it. They don't put just anybody on the cover of the *National Enquirer*!" I can't say that I appreciated my mother's cavalier attitude about the whole thing. She thought it was hilarious. By the way, later that year, I *did* meet Mike Tyson.

He did not ask me for a date.

As I mentioned earlier, I was the first Miss America to have an official platform. This became another of my responsibilities.

The Miss America Organization wanted the titleholder to use her voice and influence for social awareness and change. During that heady first week as Miss America, the organization and I developed a strategy for implementing my "Motivating Youth to Excellence" platform. I decided I wanted to speak to as many young people as possible. I spoke at schools, youth centers, youth rallies, youth ministries, and college campuses. I encouraged young people to dream big, work hard, and never give up. I used my own journey to Miss America as an example of how they could succeed against the odds.

I let elementary school kids hold and try on my crown. I talked to middle school kids about being their authentic selves. I especially loved speaking to teenagers at high schools. With them, I ventured into subjects like drug use and sexuality.

Young people more than anything want adults to be authentic. I shared with them my teenage angst and insecurities. I told them about the crushes I had on boys who didn't crush back. I talked to them about how much I wanted to be popular and accepted as a teenager. And I let them, like the younger kids, hold and try on the crown. I loved interacting with young people. They were fun, funny, challenging, and expressive.

In an effort to captivate the young audiences I addressed, I tried something I hoped would allow me to connect with them. The late 1980s and early 1990s were the golden age of hip-hop. Artists like Run DMC, Big Daddy Kane, and Rakim flooded radio waves with a tsunami of rap lyrics about life, love, and hardship. Rap had even spread to Christian music.

I'd learned a Christian rap by Stephen Wiley called "Rappin' for Jesus" when I attended a church in Columbia, Missouri. I took creative license and modified the words a bit to make it personal. Sometimes, when I was introduced to a group of students, I would get them to clap a beat in unison and I would rap, "My name is Debbye Turner. And I'm hot as a burner. And I rap to a T. So everybody that's sittin' around, stop and listen to me."

The kids would go wild. They never expected a Miss America to "spit rhymes." As the rap goes on, it talks about a real and abiding relationship with God. Its lyrics include, "Well, I love the Lord and it's all I know. I'm gonna' sing His praise everywhere I go."

While the kids loved the rap, some school administrators did not. The song is unabashedly Christian. Some non-Christians didn't like me proselytizing, as they called it. The Anti-Defamation League contacted the Miss America office and threatened to sue the organization if I didn't stop singing the Christian rap at public schools. This was the first time my faith was challenged in that way.

Miss America CEO Leonard Horn talked to me about the situation. He never forbade me from performing the rap and let me know it was ultimately my choice. I was torn. I had a First Amendment right of both freedom of speech and freedom of religion. Plus, the rap was a very effective way of grabbing the attention of young audiences, which is not always easy to do. But I didn't want to cause trouble, and I especially didn't want to get sued. I prayed fervently about the situation. And God worked it out.

I came up with a compromise, a God-inspired idea. I would not voluntarily perform the rap at schools, but if a student at a school asked me to perform it, then I would. That satisfied all parties involved. The result: at almost every school I visited for the rest of the year, someone asked me to perform the rap!

I don't believe it's my place as a Christian to force my beliefs on someone else. That's not what Jesus does. He draws us through love. I believe that if we are true to our convictions, God will open a path for our witness. When we live out the love of Jesus, then people will ask us about the source of the joy, peace, and hope they see in us. That's our open door to share the love and work of Christ in our lives.

Some of my fondest memories as Miss America included connecting with young people all over the country. I enjoyed the time I spent with them because I could let loose and be myself. Yes, they were enchanted by the crown and the title, but they had no notions about who I should be or how I should act. This gave me space to be myself.

I admitted to young people my battle with insecurity. Despite my faith, even as I had prayed and practiced and prepared to compete in pageants, I struggled with feelings of inadequacy. And I wrestled every day with self-doubt and anxiety as Miss America. Actually, I still do. The primary opposition that I have faced over my lifetime has always been a battle with insecurity. I have almost always wrestled with thoughts like,

I can't do it, I don't have it in me. Or *I'm not pretty enough, or smart enough, or strong enough.*

Moses had similar problems. Throughout the book of Exodus, Moses told God that he couldn't save the Israelites from Pharaoh because he was a stutterer. He asked God to send someone better qualified for the job. God did send Aaron along, but that did not get Moses off the hook.

Are there struggles and weaknesses that you try to hide?

How could being authentic about your human weakness liberate you from shame and guilt?

What are parts of your personality that you have masked in order to fit in?

How have you hidden true talents and passions?

God knows what He's doing when He chooses us for His divine purposes. He never, ever makes mistakes. Rest in that fact.

In fact, the most authentic thing we can do sometimes is admit our vulnerabilities. Authenticity is not about perfection. It's quite the opposite. You are not Superwoman. No one is.

Admitting our struggles can be hard and make us feel exposed. But it's also liberating. I admitted my insecurities and self-doubt when I talked to young people, especially little girls. I wanted them to understand that I was not the poster child for perfection. Authenticity in admitting our fallibilities opens the opportunity for real connection.

Dare to be truly and completely you. You will find freedom and success in your authenticity.

Often, authenticity requires accountability.

———

During my year of traveling and making appearances as Miss America, I was struggling to make time with God. I determined to do what I could. Initially, my prayer life was on the fly. My days were so long that usually once I got to my hotel room at the end of a day, I was spent. So I prayed in the shower while getting ready for the day. I prayed during car rides between events. I whispered quick prayers right before speaking engagements.

But I was constantly pouring out and not refilling. It didn't take long to become spiritually depleted.

When I spoke with my mom on the telephone, she often asked about my Bible reading and church attendance, admonishing me not to neglect being fed by the Word of God. I knew she was right. I had a responsibility to nurture my faith, regardless of the demands of my schedule.

We need people in our lives who inspire us, but also to help convict us; they motivate us to do better and live according to biblical principles. Being authentic in my faith walk during my reign as Miss America would have been impossible without being surrounded by prayer partners and wise counselors.

Who we allow around us is critically important. It determines what we are being fed. It's important to have people surrounding us who will default to prayer before advice and observation—people who tell us the truth, in love, even when we don't want to hear it, and people who will love us when we are at our best as well as when we are at our worst.

During those times when I had decided to give up on competing for Miss America, it was one of those people who encouraged me and said, "Debbye, you can't give up." Even as I initially brainstormed this book, I had accountability partners who checked on me and asked, "Debbye, have you written today? Did you contact a publisher?" We need such people who keep us on our toes.

Success is not a solitary experience. It takes a team of people around us.

While on the road as Miss America, I asked a friend from my church to send me the sermons preached each week. Once a month, I received a box of sermon tapes, my lifeline to being spiritually fed during that year. Whenever possible, I also visited churches in whatever city I happened to be in on a given Sunday. It was supremely important to find ways to feed my spirit. A former pastor of mine used to say, "If you're too busy for God, then you're too busy."

Traveling the country as Miss America was no excuse for neglecting my spiritual growth. Being Miss America could have been a justified distraction. I had prayed about winning. God allowed me to win. So, the argument could be made that God wanted me to give myself completely to the role and responsibilities of having the title. But God never wants anything in our lives to compete with Him.

Even though I had received what God had given me, He never intended for His gift to be worshipped. He wants us to worship Him and only Him. A part of the reason it took so long for me to become Miss America was my need to mature spiritually enough so that the crown would not become an idol to me. I had to minimize it, and so die spiritually to my own motives. By the time I became Miss America, I was humble and broken before the Lord. I wouldn't dare take any credit.

Seven years of competing had changed me. Those years were not only about honing my competition skills, they helped me understand that everything I had, everything I was able to do, and everywhere I was able to go was because of God's grace and blessings. I understood I was nothing without God and His saving power. I knew without a shadow of doubt that God deserved all the glory for what He'd done in my life. That's why I could not—would not—allow being Miss America to become a distraction.

Doing "all things through Christ" became my mantra as Miss America. Over the course of the year, thousands of articles were written about me in newspapers and magazines. I was on the cover of *Ebony* and *Jet* magazines and featured in *Essence* magazine, pioneering publications then that were among the first magazines to feature African American lifestyle, fashion, and celebrities and to focus on the interests of African Americans. I appeared in articles in every major newspaper in the United States. I even wrote guest columns for *USA Today* and *Good Housekeeping* magazine, to name a few.

For the most part, the media coverage I received was positive (except for the controversy over my remarks about my skin color). But very often, journalists would get some aspect of my story wrong. My name would be misspelled. Or my age or hometown would be incorrect. Every once in a while, a quote would be taken out of context that changed the meaning of what I was trying to say. Some reporters asked very personal, invasive questions, such as whether I was a virgin.

Because I was a veterinary student, I was criticized by some in the animal rights community who assumed I condoned animal experimentation. There seemed to always be some topic or issue that I had to explain or clarify. By the end of my year, I'd had my fill of press coverage. I wanted nothing more than to return to anonymity. I discovered that this wouldn't occur for several years. Unfazed, I knew I could endure. I could survive. I could do all things through Jesus Christ who strengthened me.

By the end of my year of service as Miss America, I was bone tired. All the flights, airports, speeches, autographs, interviews, photos, parades, performances, luncheons, banquets, TV appearances, and continuous smiling took their toll. For that whole year, I did not have the luxury of looking slouchy, running to the store in sweats without makeup, or just being grouchy. Perfection was the expectation; Miss America had to be perfectly put together and happy at all times. In the weeks leading up to the next Miss America pageant, I grew anxious for the next young woman to win the title and carry the mantle.

As I readied to place the crown on my successor, I reflected on the wild ride called "being Miss America." While I was still "just Debbye," I was different.

The experience did not change the core of who I am, but it did broaden my horizons. I had a voice. People knew who I was. I had the opportunity to do something with the forum God had given me. The year had been the most incredible one of my life. I visited forty of the fifty United States, traveled more than two hundred thousand air miles, and saw more hotel rooms than I care to remember. I did more in those twelve months than many do in a lifetime.

The burden of responsibility that comes with success also has its rewards.

The young girls I met along the way—who told me that they wanted to be just like me when they grew up—made the seven years and eleven tries in two states worth every minute.

The older woman at the King of Prussia Mall and the countless others who cheered me on, defended me, and prayed for me sweetened the entire fantastic experience.

The absolute thrill of the year, though, had been meeting and talking to hundreds of thousands of young people. I didn't change every life I came in contact with, but I pray I at least planted a seed in their minds to think beyond their circumstances and reach for the impossible.

I am living proof that seemingly impossible dreams do come true.

As I walked down the runway in Convention Hall one last time as the current Miss America, 357 days after I made the first walk across its famed stage, my heart was bursting with humility and appreciation. I knew with assurance that I did not become Miss America because I was the most beautiful girl competing. I was not. I didn't become Miss America because I was the most talented. I was not. I was not necessarily the most eloquent or the most intelligent, and if you don't believe me—just ask the mothers of any of the other contestants who competed with me.

I was crowned because God had a divine plan for my life. But it was a plan that required that I be authentic, not give up, learn from my shortcomings, and trust God with all my heart, mind, and strength.

Although my year as Miss America was coming to a close, God was just getting started on me.

SIX

Courage

Courage is often misunderstood. We think that those who are courageous feel no fear or hesitation. Not so. Courage is being willing to act in spite of your fear. In other words, courage is a decision, not a feeling.

Life sometimes throws us curves. Circumstances happen. God has plans that perplex us.

Perhaps you are going through a time like that right now. There is a little something to be worried about or maybe something bigger that scares you. Perhaps you are stuck in a phase of uncertainty. Maybe fear now clings to you, making it more difficult to make bold moves.

I have to tell you . . . prayer not only changes things, it changes us. Communicating with God can give you the needed courage to move on when life demands it.

As I would find out in the years following my Miss America reign, courage is a key success principle in life. We need courage to pursue our dreams. At times we need courage just to face the future. Certainly, we cannot do life without some measure of courage.

Reentry into regular life after that whirlwind year of being Miss America was almost as surreal as my Miss America year. I'd become accustomed to special treatment and perks. Flying first class on airplanes, riding in stretch limousines, and sleeping in hotel presidential suites had begun to feel normal. Because Ellie and Bonnie handled all the day-to-day drudgery like hotel check-in, hailing taxis (this was way before Uber), and paying tips to bellhops and skycaps, I'd been blissfully unaware of the actual logistics of the year.

What are you afraid of will happen if you pursue your dream?

Is your confidence (or lack thereof) in your own ability or in God's ability?

By refocusing from *can't* to *can,* how can you fearlessly pursue your dream?

So when I flew back to Missouri after I passed on the crown to the next Miss America and got a dirty look from a skycap whom I forgot to tip, I realized that being a former Miss America is very different from being the current one. No travel companion was with me to take care of it. I carried my own luggage. I started doing my own shopping. And if I wanted to get somewhere, I had to get in my car and drive myself. I missed the Miss America perks.

And to top it all off, my first class when I returned to veterinary school clinical rotations was *theriogenology,* the study of reproduction in animals. Theriogenologists are the ob-gyns of the veterinary world. It was quite a contrast to go from the glamorous world of gowns and crowns to wearing coveralls, boots, and plastic gloves that extend all the way to my shoulder.

The administration, faculty, and (most) students at my vet school had been very supportive of my pursuit of the Miss America title. The school got increased media attention after

I won. Some of that was beneficial to the school. Some of it was not. I am grateful that the school took it in stride. Overall, I welcomed the normalcy; it was a relief to not wear makeup, high heels, big hair, or a crown every day. The cows and dogs didn't care who I was.

Being back in school shielded me a bit from the white-hot media attention that I'd received the previous year. That was awesome. No more appearing in the tabloids or being ambushed by a reporter as I exited the back door of a building. For the most part, attention had shifted to the next Miss America, Marjorie Vincent, a whip-smart piano virtuoso who was kind, a bit soft-spoken, and not to be underestimated.

What got a lot of attention when I crowned Marjorie was that she, too, is African American. After its more than sixty-year history, Miss America crowned its first African American, Vanessa Williams. Suzette Charles assumed the title when Vanessa resigned. Then seven years after Vanessa's crowning, two additional African American Miss Americas in a row were crowned. It seemed times had changed, and Marjorie was up for the job.

I retreated blissfully into learning how to check a cow for pregnancy and treat piglets for diarrhea. After my theriogenology rotation, I had surgery, medical services, and radiology clinical rotations. I was happy to be finishing up my last six months of veterinary school. It was a long, tough road, especially since I juggled it while competing in pageants.

I did not graduate at the top of my class. But I was also not at the bottom. I was grateful to earn my Doctor of Veterinary Medicine degree. I started joking that I was no longer Miss America. I was now Dr. America.

Soon after finishing veterinary school, I started a position with the Ralston Purina pet food company as a spokesperson for "Caring for Pets," its new pet education campaign.

It was the perfect job for me.

It entailed doing media interviews across the country about being a responsible pet owner. I did radio interviews, television appearances, and speeches. It was just like being Miss America, only now I was talking about animals as a veterinary expert. There was no crown or limousine, but the schedule and responsibilities were very familiar. I enjoyed the next two years that I spent promoting the program.

The pet education position allowed me to continue doing other speaking engagements. So I continued speaking to young people. And I began giving speeches to community organizations, women's groups, and veterinarians. For five years after I graduated from veterinary school, I was a motivational speaker. There was enough demand to allow me to speak full-time. I gave two hundred speeches a year on average. So in some respects, my Miss America year continued for several years. And I loved it.

But, because I went straight back to veterinary school after my Miss America year, then back on the road speaking and promoting the Caring for Pets program, I didn't really take a break. I was like the Energizer bunny, and my schedule took its toll.

Unlike the Energizer bunny, I began to lose steam. Physically exhausted and emotionally depleted, I eventually didn't want to be around people. I didn't want to smile. I didn't want to have to meet people's expectations. The most draining part of being Miss America was trying to live up to what they thought Miss America should be. I felt pressured to be funny, smart, gracious, tireless, compassionate, entertaining; all while wearing a smile and five-inch heels.

When I wasn't at a speaking engagement or doing a media tour for Caring for Pets, I retreated to my home, far away from the expectations. I needed to detox from all the attention. I spent the day in my pajamas, only getting off the couch to use the bathroom or grab something to eat. I didn't open my blinds. I didn't answer the phone.

Whenever I could, I shut myself inside my house and hid from life.

I relished the solitude. But the more I holed up in my home, the less I wanted to go back out into the world and live the big, bright life that had become my reality. Occasionally I canceled a speaking engagement because I just didn't have the energy to meet the commitment. The more I stayed on the couch, the more I wanted to stay on the couch. It became harder and harder to get up and get moving again.

I didn't realize it at the time, but I was depressed.

At that time, I thought I was merely very tired. But I'd lost motivation to keep pushing as hard as I'd done during my year as Miss America and even the final year of veterinary school. As I laid on the couch eating junk food and watching hours and hours of television, I felt ashamed. I felt like a fraud.

I was supposed to be Miss America—charming, witty, inspirational. But I felt defeated, unworthy, useless. And alone.

I didn't tell anyone how I really felt. How could I? People saw me as an accomplished, successful person. The thought of bursting their bubble made me feel even worse. I was in a toxic spiral. The more I isolated myself, the worse I felt. The worse I felt, the more I isolated myself.

It's in that place of isolation that the enemy of our soul can do the most damage. When we get into a barren place like that and allow no one in, there is no counterbalance to all the negative, crushing thoughts that seek to kill our spirit. That's why it's so important to stay connected to trusted (especially *praying*) friends or family who can speak encouragement and hope into our lives.

In those darkest moments, we really don't want to hear anyone tell us that "it's going to be OK."

But it *is* going to be OK.

And when we are at our lowest, that's when we need to hear that truth the most. When we are at our weakest, it's imperative that we use even our last ounce of strength to push ourselves toward hearing the Word of God, praying or asking someone to pray with and for us, and being in the fellowship of other believers. There is safety and encouragement in that fellowship.

My mom told me often when I was growing up that when I least wanted to go to church is exactly when I most needed to go. I live by that to this day. Even when I didn't feel any huge change in my heart and mind after the service, seeds of hope and life were planted. Plus, I succeeded in getting off the couch . . . *that* was half the battle.

Another battle was coming that I would have never predicted. One day, a seemingly ordinary phone call with my mom turned ominous. She shared with me that she hadn't been feeling well. For my mother to even make such an admission was totally out of character. She was always making faith-filled confessions: "I am blessed," "I've got the victory," or "All is well." These were just a few of her quick replies when someone asked her how she was doing.

During this particular call, I could tell that she was not her normal, bubbly self. She wasn't quizzing me about every minute detail of my life. She was not inquiring about my spiritual growth. She seemed off her game, and I became very concerned. After asking her several specific questions about how she was *really* feeling, I declared that she needed to go see her doctor. She agreed. That worried me more. Ordinarily, she would never concede to seeing a doctor. Something was definitely wrong. We learned soon after she saw her primary care physician that my mom had a mass in her reproductive tract. A specialist confirmed that it was cancer. And it was malignant.

A treatment plan of high doses of radiation was quickly established. My mother had to travel to Memphis, Tennessee, an hour's drive from Jonesboro, to get the radiation treatments. Her tumor was large, so the radiation was intense. It drained her of energy. She lost that glow in her skin and that twinkle in her eyes. It was hard to watch her go through that harrowing process. But we were more than hopeful; we were filled with faith, expecting a miracle.

Of course, prayer was the foundation of our approach to her treatment. Friends and family around the country joined us in prayer. I had no doubt that God would heal her. As the radiation did its work on the cancer, it also greatly damaged the surrounding normal tissue. Over time, she was in a lot of pain, including when she stood or walked. But I was convinced that the treatment would be successful, my mom would soon be cancer-free, and she would live for many years to come.

People regularly visited my mom and held prayer vigils. A few times, the intercessors would pray all night long at her house. As I traveled around the country, speaking at churches, I would ask those congregations to pray for her. I was concerned because my mom's treatment was taking its toll; she wasn't eating much, she was lethargic, and she didn't understand how or why she had cancer.

When I was home for a visit or took her to the hospital for her radiation treatments, I watched my mom cry out to God for deliverance and healing. In her prayer time, she often asked God what she had done wrong to bring this on herself. She repeatedly repented, in case she had somehow fallen short of God's expectations. That troubled me greatly.

I knew my mom and her character. While she certainly was not perfect, she was as close to it as anyone I'd ever encountered. She prayed hours a day, read her Bible almost constantly. She barely took time to watch television. When she wasn't working, she was on the phone praying with someone or counseling people through their difficulties. She visited the sick. She cooked for the elderly. She freely gave of her possessions and her life to those in need. If anyone "deserved" to be healed, it was my mom.

Her deep faith in God and love for Him informed these actions. She staunchly believed God wants us to stay in close relationship to Him *and* care about people and their needs.

While Scripture does not promise a healing for so-called "deserving" people, particularly those known for good works, it does promise healing. I trusted God could restore Mommy's health. And because she had brought me up believing in a loving God who is also a healer, I couldn't understand why she kept asking God to forgive her. Finally, I couldn't take it.

"Mommy, you've got to stop this," I said, during a visit in summer 1994. "You haven't done anything wrong. I don't know why God allowed you to go through this, but I know He is not punishing you. He's not that kind of God. That's what you've taught me all my life!"

We prayed together and I went off to bed. The next day, I awakened to the sound of my mom praying in the living room. Lying in my bed, listening to Mommy seek God had been a normal and frequent occurrence my entire life. It was comforting and encouraging. Her faith-filled prayers were the true soundtrack of my childhood.

Something had changed overnight. On this morning, I did not hear my mom begging God to tell her what she did wrong or to forgive her for some unknown sin. I heard her praising and worshipping God between winces of pain.

"God, I thank You," she moaned.

"God, I trust You," she groaned.

"God, you are awesome," she sighed.

"God, you are mighty," she affirmed.

Even though she was suffering physically, with all her might she worshipped God. I began to worship God along with her from my bed. As she praised God for His goodness, I thanked Him for His faithfulness.

I don't know if my mom ever knew I was listening and joining her in prayer. But she taught me yet another valuable lesson that day. God is worthy of praise no matter what circumstance we find ourselves in. Through her pain, my mom praised almighty God. I imagine this must have been close to how Job felt when he declared, "Though He slay me, yet will I trust Him" (Job 13:15 NKJV).

Mommy suffered severe complications from the radiation. She had to go to another specialist to consider how to address those. I canceled some commitments and drove home to Jonesboro to take her to the new specialist in Memphis. The consultation went well. The doctor recommended surgery, optimistic about a favorable outcome. Encouraged, my mother was happier than I'd seen her in a long while. As we headed back to Jonesboro, although she was still in enormous pain, she was smiling and looked forward to the surgery bringing some relief. I was relieved too. We could finally see the light at the end of this terrible tunnel.

I remember clearly that this was a Wednesday afternoon. Initially, I'd planned to stay another couple of days to help my mom around the house, but the surgery was scheduled for the next week. Since I would need to return to Jonesboro to be with my mom during the surgery, I decided to cut this visit short. My plan was to return to St. Louis, where I lived at the time, and get some things done in order to be free to return the following week. Plus, I had a speaking engagement scheduled on the coming Sunday and had planned to return to Jonesboro after that to take my mom to the hospital for the necessary preoperative tests. The plan was all set in my mind.

Mommy was disappointed I was leaving early, but she understood. Quickly packing my suitcase to get on the road for the four-hour drive to St. Louis, I kissed her, told her I loved her, and promised to return. Her split-level house had a set of stairs descending from the living room down to the front door. I see this scene in my mind as though it happened yesterday. Mommy sat on the couch, across the living room from the staircase. She wore a comfy nightgown. As I went downstairs toward the front door, she asked me a question.

I stopped about two steps down from the top and looked at her. I could tell by the expression on her face that she really didn't want me to leave. I answered her question and reassured her that everything was going to be OK. I reminded her what the doctor had told her about the success of the scheduled procedure. I smiled, told her again that I loved her and would call when I got home to let her know that I made it safely. She smiled back and told me that she loved me.

I made it back to St. Louis without incident. Over the next couple of days, I attended to the drudgeries: bills, opening mail, and grocery shopping. Friday night I called Mommy to check on her. We chatted about unremarkable things. It was late and I was tired. I told her that I was going to hang up. She didn't want to end the conversation. "No, don't go. Let's talk some more," she said.

Frankly, I didn't have anything else to talk about. We sat silently on the phone for a couple of minutes.

"Mommy, get some rest. I am going to bed. I will call you tomorrow."

"I love you," we said to each other, ending the call.

———

Saturday came and went in a flurry of activity, and I never got around to calling Mommy, but resolved to call her the next day. Sunday, I was the guest speaker at a church in the St. Louis area. I don't remember the specifics of the service. I just wanted to get home quickly to begin packing for my trip back to Jonesboro. I stopped at a gas station on my way home from the church to fill the tank in preparation for the drive. While the gas tank was filling, my cell phone rang. I ducked my head into the driver's-side door to reach my phone. It was my mother's best friend, Dorothy Brown, on the line.

I answered, "Hey, Dorothy! What's up?"

Dorothy did not call me often, but it was not totally unusual. She checked on my mom and helped her when my sister and I were not in town. I figured she was calling to tell me some reminder or to-do item when I got to Jonesboro the next day. As soon as I heard her voice, I knew something was very wrong.

"Debbye!" she almost shouted. Then her voice wavered. "Oh, Debbye. I'm at your mom's house." She sighed heavily. "Debbye, the coroner is here."

That made no sense. *Why would a coroner be at my mom's house? Did he stop by for my mom to pray with him?*

"What? What do you mean, Dorothy?" I answered with a growing knot in my stomach.

"She's gone, Debbye. Your mom's dead."

I almost blacked out. But I was standing at a gas pump. I had to keep it together, at least long enough to get home. I calmly asked Dorothy if she had laid hands on my mother and asked God to raise her from the dead. I know that might sound bizarre, but that's the kind of faith I have in God. And He's done it before, so why not now?

I may have even sounded unstable to Dorothy, who informed me she had not prayed for Mommy. I firmly instructed her to get off the phone and go lay hands on my mother. To her credit, she didn't argue with me. She said that she would. I told Dorothy that I was on my way home and would call her when I got there.

I removed the gas nozzle from my car, got in the car, and slowly drove home. I think I held my breath the entire way. I knew that I couldn't fall apart yet. I needed to get home safely.

I needed to return Dorothy's call. And I needed to call my sister. I had to keep my wits about me.

I called Dorothy back. "Did you pray for Mommy? Is she breathing?" I asked with the utmost sincerity.

She confirmed my mother was still dead. That's when I lost it. I hung up and crumbled to the floor, wailing.

"God, this was not supposed to happen!" I railed.

He was supposed to heal her. She was supposed to be OK. Her pre-op tests were scheduled for the very next day. Surely God could have sustained her for just one more day. I was shocked. The doctors said that the cancer was gone. We just needed to fix the damage done by the radiation. This was not supposed to happen!

The hardest conversations I have ever had in my life were the calls I had to make to my sister and my maternal grandmother to tell them that Mommy had died. It was awful. Of course, they were devastated. We all were.

The grief of losing my mother was a distinct physical pain. My body hurt. My mind ached. My thoughts spun out of control. I kept replaying that last doctor's visit, the last time I saw my mom, the last time I talked to her. I wondered what I should have done differently. Curiously, for a long time afterwards, I thought my mom's death was somehow my fault.

If I hadn't left early on that last trip, maybe it wouldn't have happened. If I had stayed on the phone with her on that last call, maybe the outcome would be different. If I'd prayed more, read my Bible more, went to church more. What if. What if. What if. I was in utter disbelief. How could my vivacious, praying, kind, generous, anointed, bigger-than-life mom die? It just didn't make any sense.

I know I'm not alone. Many people similarly feel responsible for a loved one's death. It's an unreasonable feeling born out of debilitating grief. Thankfully, God helps us to see the truth. Mommy's death was the first time I'd believed God for something this significant and it didn't happen the way I prayed. I was surprised as well as devastated. Mommy's death shook my confidence in the goodness of God—not in His existence but in His temperament.

Are you really a good Father? I wondered. *What kind of God are you if this is how you treat people who dedicate their lives to you? How close do I really want to get to you if this is how you treat your children?*

I didn't question the existence of God. I just didn't care much for His ways. But even in this broken state, all I knew to do was to pray. Prayer was the only real survival skill that my mother had taught me. So I prayed. But they were not flowery, sweet-nothings prayers. I grew up in a time when many Christians believed that we are not supposed to question God or express feelings of frustration toward Him. But the truth is, I was mad at God. I felt like He had let me down. The most important step that I could take at that moment was to be honest with myself and God.

My mom had taught me that prayer is open, honest communication with God. She had encouraged me to share my feelings with Him regardless of the circumstances. My mom was a counselor. And as such, she had shared with me the importance of also being honest with myself. Faced with her death and my overwhelming grief, I had to act on those lessons.

I had to courageously admit to the Lord how I really felt. I poured out my heart to God, sharing all the grief, disappointment, disillusionment, and pain. I defiantly told God that I could not walk this journey on my own. I needed Him. Even though I didn't particularly like Him at the moment, I had enough sense to know that I needed Him. I remembered my mother worshipping God while in her pain and misery. I was determined to do the same.

One night, I couldn't go to sleep because of the horror of my mom's death. My prayers seemed to be hitting the ceiling and falling back down around me. Since they didn't seem to be getting through to God, I decided to read the Bible. I couldn't think of a Scripture, so I picked up the Bible and let it fall open randomly. I closed my eyes, pointed my index finger, and let it fall to a spot on the page.

I opened my eyes and my gaze fell on: "Be anxious for nothing, but in everything by prayer and supplication, with thanksgiving, let your requests be made known to God; and the peace of God, which surpasses all understanding, will guard your hearts and minds through Christ Jesus" (Philippians 4:6–7 NKJV). That's what I needed—peace.

"God, I need that peace," I prayed. "Please give me that peace."

Soon, I drifted off to sleep with the Bible resting on my chest, still open to Philippians 4. When I woke up the next morning, I felt peace like I'd never experienced it before in my life. A peace that defied my own comprehension. I can't explain it with human understanding. It truly was a peace that surpassed all my understanding.

***

We tend to think of courage as standing in battle, strong and fearless, facing the enemy with a sword and fierce defiance.

But courage comes in different forms.

It takes courage to get help for depression.

It takes courage to overcome addictions.

It takes courage to risk failure.

It takes courage to trust.

It takes courage to face loss and go through grief.

Every life faces a battle with something. Every person looks tragedy in the eye and must find a way of dealing with it. The mark of a successful person is not in a life free of these challenges but in facing them bravely with a courage that comes from God.

What battle are you facing right now?

How have you turned to God to sustain you through this?

———

I exhausted myself trying to avoid the grief of losing my mom. I admitted to God that I needed His help; I couldn't bear the pain on my own. Just the admission of the need for help was all that was necessary for God to begin doing what only He can do. God promises that He comes when we call on Him. He hears our prayer and leads us to the next step of our healing journey. I was led to counseling.

The weariness that I'd been feeling after my year as Miss America combined with the crushing weight of my mother's death became more than I could bear. I could not take a deep breath, square my shoulders, and pull myself out of the funk by sheer force of will. I needed help.

I began meeting with a Christian counselor to help me process my feelings of grief and despair—and to get help with depression. Because my mother was a counselor by profession, she had encouraged me to identify and express my emotions throughout my childhood. I was not averse to getting counseling. I am grateful that because of my upbringing, there was no stigma about counseling for me.

Part of the weight of struggling with depression was the feeling that I was the only one experiencing that spiral. I thought no one else who had achieved some level of success struggled to maintain that feeling of being successful. In admitting my struggle to my counselor, I discovered I was not alone; lots of people deal with this. Just knowing that I was not unique in this challenge was comforting. It helped me persevere through the pain. Many of us become debilitated in our struggle because we don't realize that others have experienced the same thing. We're not failures. We're not freaks. We're human. And in our humanness, we need a supernatural God. The isolation is as harmful as the depression or anguish.

Isolation can be worse in an age of social media, where idealized, filtered, highlight-reel versions of people's lives bombard our devices. It looks like everyone else is living the good life. The truth is, nobody's life is that perfect. I am not knocking social media, but I *am* making the point that if we are not careful, we can buy into a deceptive narrative that will cause great harm to our minds and emotions.

So the question becomes, in our normal humanness, what will we allow God to do in our lives? God brought me through this dark period and through many tough circumstances since. I have no doubt that He will bring you through as well. *If* you allow Him to. And if you disregard the opinions of others who don't have divine knowledge of what will work for *you*.

Having a counselor who would present biblical perspectives and pray with me was important to me. The process pushed me to be honest about how I really felt. That was the first step toward healing and deliverance. In order to be in real relationship with God, we must worship Him "in spirit and truth" (John 4:24 NKJV). We can't be in a truthful, intimate relationship with God without being honest with ourselves. It's only in that place of authenticity that a door is open for Him to come in. He won't participate in our masquerading.

I kept a journal in those early days after my mom's death. "God, I am mad at you. I don't understand you," I wrote. The act of expressing those emotions on paper started the healing process. It was important to get them out in the open. I also asked God questions in my journal. "God, how am I going to move forward with my life without my mom?" "What do I do next?"

A process of transparency with God propels us forward. It's important to keep moving forward even in our pain. Over time, as I continued to pour out my heart in the journal and ask God questions, He responded. Sometimes even as I wrote the question, I would begin to sense Him dealing with my heart. Thus, journaling became an avenue to rebuild my trust in God.

God never intended for us to live permanently in our "wilderness." Just like He didn't intend for the children of Israel to live permanently in the wilderness after He brought them out of Egypt. The harsh difficulties of the wilderness were supposed to be temporary. There was a promised land waiting for them (Numbers 33). And there is a promise of healing, wholeness, and victory waiting for us.

To face grief courageously, it's absolutely essential not to pitch a tent in the place of our anguish. God never intended for us to live in that place permanently. We must trust the Lord to bring us *through* our wilderness season. It's temporary. So don't get comfortable in your pain.

Keep seeking God. Letting prayer partners and trusted believers into our place of despair is key to momentum. My close friends, my pastor, and mentors who were prayer support were key to my healing. I had to allow others to speak life and truth into me. Christian counseling, praying with friends, going to church, and Bible study were critical.

Some of the despair that we feel when dealing with loss is because we don't see our way forward. We can't imagine how life will be without that loved one, or without that relationship, job, or position. We create a context in which that person or that place in life defines who we are and our future. And when we lose that person or place, part of the grief is that we no longer have that context. We wonder, *What do I do now? How will I make it?*

One aspect of grief is not being able to see the path ahead in this "new normal." I found that some of my healing came by trusting God to show me how to move forward; to show me what I should do next in a life that didn't include my mother being with me physically on this earth. Some of my dismay at her loss was alleviated as I began to take baby steps. Living without her wasn't what I wanted or ever imagined, but I was learning that I could do it.

I could seek God for answers about my life without first going to my mom. I could pray through situations on my own. And God began to send people into my life to walk alongside me. My mother was no longer on earth with me, but God supplied the motherly counsel and nurturing that I needed through other people. When we experience loss, God always provides what we need, even more than we had before. When we learn to trust in God's provision for our lives, losses in life sometimes lead to other gains.

However, it has not been my experience that God just magically lays out a road map for life, like following the "yellow brick road." But His Word is a "lamp" to our feet (Psalm 119:105). Although we face an unknown future, God is faithful to show us that next step. When reeling from the pain of loss, we can trust God to help us take the next step. Don't worry about next week or next year. Just take the next step.

For many, that seems impossible. The pain is too great. The trust in God seems broken. That's OK. Let God into the place where you are right now—into the brokenness. Acknowledge your hurt. Acknowledge your pain. Acknowledge your disappointment. And ask God to come into that space where you are now. He will. We don't have to find God. Many people struggle because they feel as if they have to conduct an epic search for God, as if He's lost somewhere. Others lose hope because they feel He's playing hide-and-seek at their expense.

God is not like that. He is ready and willing to help us. We just have to call to Him in prayer. And He comes to us . . . wherever we are. When God enters a space, He changes it. So when we let Him into our pain, we change simply because of God's presence. I changed—for the better.

That's why, despite the pain and despair I experienced after being Miss America and losing my mom, I would not want to change any of it. The dark times were scary. But the light did come. And I am better for it. My relationship with God is far more mature, stronger now *because* I don't have Mommy to run to when I need an answer from God.

I had to learn how to seek God and listen for His voice on my own. Honestly, I was a spiritual teenager. As a grown woman naturally, I was stuck in an underdeveloped place spiritually because my mom and her relationship with God was my safety net. I felt that if I couldn't get an answer from God, she could. So sometimes I wouldn't try that hard, knowing that my mom would stand in the gap. But as my mother told me when I was seven years old, at our kitchen table, I couldn't get into heaven on her apron string, and I was still holding on to it.

Her death meant that I *had* to seek God on my own. I *had* to learn how to step out on faith based on what I knew about the Bible. I had to search Scripture for what God has to say about my life, instead of calling my mom and asking her what God had to say about this or that. My mom's absence forced me to finally and truly have my own relationship with God without her as a go-between. As a result, my walk with God grew deeper and richer.

Seeking God on my own didn't mean I didn't need other

people though. As I kept praying, there were times when I received counseling, and leaned on accountability partners who helped me stay on track.

Courage to work through my grief ushered me into opportunities that I never dreamed of and allowed me to discover God's further purposes for my life.

SEVEN

Purpose

I'm often asked about purpose—how to identify it and how to wholeheartedly pursue it. My answer? Divine passion leads to divine purpose. For me, living out my divine purposes started with an intense interest and passion for something.

Take a good look at what you're passionate about, about the activities or people toward which you naturally gravitate. There's a good chance that God's purpose lies somewhere in those.

Of course, not every desire is from God, but if we attune our hearts to the Lord, I believe that we will discover our God-given passions. When we pursue them, they lead us right into our purpose.

Being Miss America wasn't on my radar as a child growing up in Jonesboro. Back then I was unaware that it was part of God's purpose for my life.

As I competed in pageants, won Miss America, and lived out my year by faith, I realized God had other purposes for me beyond that. I began to discover them as I pursued my interests and explored professions that excited me.

God creates us with His divine purpose in mind. He places in us the passion and gifts necessary to fulfill His purpose. Ultimately, the key for us as we pursue our passion is to remain open to what God is telling us about His divine purposes for our lives.

Which groups of people do you naturally gravitate to?

How could you use your gifts and talents to meet their needs while pursuing purpose?

By refocusing from a singular *purpose* to *divine purposes,* how might you say yes to new opportunities?

Many of us don't initially understand the full measure of our purpose on earth. Rather, purpose is often revealed to us in seasons or portions as life progresses. As we seek God diligently, He will reveal to us what we should know for any given season. He will reveal it to you in His time.

If you feel like you're too old or have let too much time pass to claim the purpose for which God created you, don't worry. There is still time and hope. We serve a God who created and controls time. He can redeem the time that we think we've lost.

For God, time is nothing. He's not restricted to time, or our timelines. We could be off track for five minutes or five years, but God can make that time work for our good.

Part of my divine purpose began to reveal itself very early in my life. As a little girl, I was intensely curious about how things worked. I once tried to disassemble the toaster to figure out how it browned my bread. I picked my scabs because I was fascinated with how the body heals itself and I wanted to watch the process up close. I didn't know it then, but what I really loved was science, the exploration of our world and how it works.

I also loved animals. That love came from my mom. She had a soft heart toward any abandoned, injured, half-dead creature that needed help. We would often pull over while traveling by car to help a turtle safely cross the road or pick up an injured animal and bring it home to rehabilitate. We were the neighborhood humane society. We had more cats than I care to admit. At various times, we also had dogs, turtles, fish, and birds.

Sadly, the birds and cats did not live together in harmony. Apparently to our cats, the beautiful caged parakeets in our home were fair game, no different than the birds flying around outside. Neither the parakeets nor their cage were a match for a couple of my cats who were superior hunters. After two tragic incidents, I stopped asking for birds, hoping to prevent another bird's violent end.

I always cried when I saw an animal get hurt, even in movies or on television shows. I wanted to know how to help them. I cried uncontrollably when an animal died on film or in real life. Westerns and *Bambi* almost did me in.

The combination of a love of science and a love of animals added up to veterinary medicine for me. The beauty of divine purpose is that those same factors may lead to a different path for someone else. That's why it's important to seek God's direction, while not comparing ourselves to other people. When we do compare ourselves and take actions to be more like other people, we may find ourselves outside God's purpose.

With our vast collection of pets, we spent a lot of time at the local animal clinic. I so admired our veterinarian, Dr. Jack Jones, that my mom suggested I ask if I could hang around his clinic to learn more about his job. At thirteen years old, I spent the summer watching and marveling at Dr. Jones's compassion, expertise, and commitment. By the end of the summer, I knew I wanted to be a veterinarian. I went to the library to find out just how one becomes a veterinarian. This was long before Google and the Internet.

I looked up the term *veterinary medicine* in the card catalog, the prevailing method for locating books and other library resources. On card after card, I found the name "American Veterinary Medical Association." I looked up the address for that official-sounding group and sent it a letter, explaining my love for animals and my desire to be an animal doctor. To my surprise and delight, they sent me a big packet of information containing details about locations of veterinary schools, what classes I would have to take and the grades I'd need to achieve to apply, and how long it would take to get through veterinary school. I used that information as a career road map.

By the time I reached high school, I was very focused. I took all the advanced science courses I could. I joined leadership and civic clubs. I worked toward having a good enough academic record to be accepted into veterinary school and increase the likelihood of earning academic scholarships to help my family pay for the pricey education.

I also started working the day I turned sixteen. My first job, really, was delivering newspapers when I was twelve years old, but that was short-lived. On my sixteenth birthday, I marched right down to McDonald's and got a job serving burgers. And that's when I started competing in the Miss America Scholarship pageant, a leading source of scholarships for women.

As a college student at Arkansas State University, I majored in agriculture to prepare me for veterinary school. I took physics, chemistry, organic chemistry, comparative anatomy, and many other rigorous courses. Also, in order to be considered for some vet schools, I had to take the two standardized tests required to get into medical schools: Medical College Admissions Test (MCAT) and the Veterinary College Admissions Test (VCAT). Halfway through my junior year in college, I started applying to veterinary schools. I applied to three: Louisiana State University, Kansas State University, and University of Missouri–Columbia.

I first received notification of acceptance from University of Missouri, though it only offered me a small scholarship, which wasn't even enough to pay for books. Then I received an acceptance letter from Louisiana State University, which offered me a full scholarship. The trouble was that I really wanted to go to the University of Missouri. So, at my mom's advice, I told the dean at University of Missouri about the scholarship offer from Louisiana. I asked him if there was any way the vet school could increase its scholarship offer. To my thrilled surprise, it did. The amount didn't cover all my expenses, but it helped a lot.

Veterinary school is a four-year program, just like medical school. In fact, we learn everything a human physician learns, except they just learn about one mammal, the human. Veterinarians must learn about *six* mammals (cats, dogs, horses, cows, pigs, and chickens). School was tough. I got very little sleep, spent up to twenty hours a day in class and labs, and lived off fast food. There were many days that I wanted to give up and go home. But by God's grace, after my year off as Miss America, I made it through. I graduated from the University of Missouri College of Veterinary Medicine in May 1991.

In my final year of veterinary school, as my classmates began to apply for jobs at veterinary clinics around the country, I knew that I was not going to go into private practice after I graduated. At least not right away. It was hard to explain at the time why I would spend four years of my life getting a very difficult, intense education only to not use it. All I knew was that God had something else in store for me. At the time, I had no idea what that would be. I just knew that my path was going to be atypical.

A phone call from Dr. Paul King, a veterinarian and corporate executive, solidified my plan. He told me that he worked for the pet food company Ralston Purina and wanted to talk to me about a potential opportunity. At the time, I had no idea what he had in mind, but it sounded intriguing. We scheduled a meeting, and my career trajectory changed.

At the meeting Dr. King told me about a new community education program about responsible pet ownership that Purina wanted to sponsor. The company was looking for a spokesperson to carry that message. This was just six months after I completed my year of service. Since my name recognition on the heels of my year as Miss America was quite high, and I was about to complete my Doctor of Veterinary Medicine degree, company executives felt I was the perfect choice for the job.

As Dr. King explained their vision, I knew this was what I was supposed to do. With a team of advisors from a public relations firm, we developed a program called "Caring for Pets." The program's goals were to encourage people to take good care of their pets and to teach them the great responsibility of having a pet. It also encouraged a passion for animal welfare. For two years following vet school, I traveled to dozens of American cities doing television, newspaper, radio, and magazine interviews about Caring for Pets. It was the perfect marriage of my recent experience as Miss America and my education as a veterinarian.

It also allowed me to continue doing the motivational speaking that I had begun during my year as Miss America. That was quite a wild time in my life. Even though I was no longer the reigning Miss America, I was still doing approximately two hundred speaking engagements a year.

While I was doing one of the many television interviews about the Caring for Pets program, a television agent happened to see my performance. Out of the blue, I got a phone call from a woman with a distinctive voice and a very unusual name, Babette Perry. Babette told me that she was a broadcast agent, and she believed I could have a successful career in television.

At that time, I was being approached by a whole host of people promising me the moon and the pie-in-the-sky, so I had become reasonably skeptical when someone wanted to make me "rich and famous," or "the next best thing since sliced bread." Not only was I skeptical, I was not interested. My life was full and my schedule was jam-packed. And I did not have a great love for the news media. I felt that I had not always been fairly treated by the media while I was Miss America.

Babette called me several times, trying to convince me to take her on as my agent. I finally agreed to let her find some television opportunities for me. She did. My first television job with Babette as my agent was hosting a national television special about weddings. The subject matter was not exactly in my wheelhouse, but the experience was a lot of fun.

Next, I was hired as a reporter for a pet show on PBS called *The Gentle Doctor*, and a year or two later, I was hired to *host* the show. At the same time, I started doing segments on the local news in St. Louis about pets and pet care. The experience was quite fun and exciting. In the back of my mind, I figured this "TV thing" would last for a few years, then I would go back to veterinary medicine. I never imagined that I would have a nearly twenty-five-year career in broadcast journalism.

And this was an opportunity I had almost missed.

Early on in my television career, even though I greatly enjoyed the work, I felt guilty about not practicing veterinary medicine. I'd invested a lot of time, energy, and money into getting that very difficult education in a very noble profession. I felt like I was letting down my professors, advisors, even the veterinary profession. I confided in Dr. King from Ralston Purina about my conflicted feelings. He listened intently, then told me not to worry. He said that the opportunities in my path were unique and probably short-lived.

"Debbye, you can do more good for animals giving good advice to millions of people on television than you ever could by spaying one dog at a time," he said.

Those words set me free from guilt. His affirmation was just what I needed to move forward without hesitation. It liberated me from the confines of my childhood dream, helping me see a much bigger picture of what a career in veterinary medicine could entail. My vision for my life and future broadened.

Without those affirming words from Dr. King, I might have pursued a more traditional career path in veterinary medicine, if for no other reason than a sense of guilt. After the time and money invested in my education, I felt a sense of obligation to practice medicine. The obligation could have robbed me of some pretty wonderful opportunities that would come later. I may have turned down the television opportunities out of a sense of duty to the education that I received, the professors who afforded me that education, and the profession that embraced me as a veterinarian. That would have been noble, but shortsighted.

Practicing as a veterinarian was what I *wanted* to do, but it was not what I was *called* to do. It was not my divine purpose. If we cling too tightly to only what we want, we may miss what we are called to. And we will never encounter God's true purpose for our lives.

As we seek our divine purpose, we must resist the urge to live our lives based on someone else's expectations—especially those that are contrary to the divine passion that God has placed within us.

Other people's expectations may hold you back. Only you can live your life. I know of doctors and lawyers who pursued those professions because their parents expected it of them. They are wealthy, successful, and miserable. It's not the life or purpose for which they had passion.

God's purpose is freedom. People's expectations of us can be bondage.

After speaking with Dr. King, I plunged into a new career. I figured I would ride the wave of TV opportunities for as long as they lasted. Then I would return to my veterinary aspirations.

After traveling and speaking full-time for nearly five years, I got another unexpected phone call. The owner of a local television station wanted to meet with me. At the meeting, I learned that the owner wanted to put me on contract with the station. The contract's compensation was quite generous, but there was a catch. The owner didn't have a specific job or show in mind for me; instead, the contract would just serve as a "hold" until the station came up with a plan. Its terms stipulated that I would not be able to work for any other television station in town during the term of the contract.

In essence, the agreement was free money. I didn't have to do anything necessarily. But I also couldn't consider other TV opportunities. I was tempted. Who wouldn't accept a good sum of money for doing nothing? But something didn't feel right about it. I kept pressing the owner to provide details on what my expected role would be. He would not—could not—be any more specific. During my prayer time, I just couldn't get a go-ahead in my heart to accept the offer, so I turned it down. It was risky to let the opportunity slip away, but I couldn't get peace about it. I walked away in faith.

About a week later, I received another call from a different local television station executive. The president of the NBC affiliate KSDK was planning a new show and needed male and female cohosts. I was still considered a high-profile personality at the time, so I guess he thought my "celebrity" status could be a plus for the new show. We had a meeting and he offered me the job. But, unlike the TV offer that I'd walked away from a mere week earlier, this was a real job with a multiyear contract that was worth thirty times more money.

If I had accepted the seemingly lucrative "free money" contract, I would not have been able to consider this far more appealing offer. I would have been bound by that other contract and would have missed out on KSDK's opportunity, which ultimately launched me into a new career.

Success in life is not only about finding our purpose but about finding the purpose God has for us. Usually there is a *big* difference between the two.

Don't wonder about what God wants you to do. And don't rely solely on people's opinions or encouraging words. Ask *Him*. Ask *Him* to show you *His* purpose for your life. And prepare to be surprised.

Often, God's purpose goes against what is the obvious choice. That was the case when I received that first offer from the local TV station.

When I acted in faith on what did not make complete sense in the natural, God stepped in to produce a supernatural result. As my career in television developed, I learned to earnestly seek God's direction when each new opportunity came my way.

I think it's important to realize that the enemy often throws "opportunities" our way in order to derail us from God's purpose. Throughout my life, what I call "counterfeits" have presented themselves just before the real deal, purpose-driven opportunity God had for me. Before almost every big break I received in my career, an opportunity arose that looked good, but turned out later to be a counterfeit. Making the right choice required seeking God for direction and discernment to avoid accepting the counterfeit.

If you become blinded, enamored by the natural circumstances around you, you'll miss out on God's real blessing. That's why being led by the Spirit of God is so important. Don't take anything that comes your way just because it initially seems good.

Accepting the host and reporter role at KSDK required a complete shift in my life direction. While I had lots of experience in being on television before that job, I had never worked as a real journalist. I had to learn how to find stories, research topics, get interviews, and write and edit copy that would be engaging and compelling for viewers. Obviously, people go to college and get degrees in these skills, so my learning curve was quite steep. Knowing how to spay a dog didn't help me at all.

My whole life, I had been a science geek. Creative writing was not my strength and it showed in those early stories that I reported. I looked for coaches and mentors at KSDK to help me develop my hosting and reporting skills. Man, did I need mentoring. Over time, I became friends with experienced, talented reporters and producers at the station who graciously gave me advice and direction. I opened myself to constructive criticism.

My experience in the Miss America system was the perfect preparation for my career in television. In the pageant, I learned to admit when I didn't know something and find someone who possessed the knowledge that I lacked. I matured so that I could withstand critique and use the knowledge gained to help me improve. Everyone has an opinion when you're on television. In broadcast news, there is also a constant stream of criticism from supervisors and executive producers, the viewing audience, not to mention family members and friends. Knowing how to take correction was key to my survival. I could handle the criticism in television because I'd learned how to handle it while competing in pageants. You never know when your current challenges are teaching you to handle future hurdles.

———

Having mentors is absolutely crucial to success in life. We need people to help us when we make mistakes, or to help us avoid particular mistakes altogether. At every news organization where I was employed, I identified experienced colleagues who were very good at what they did, and developed relationships with them so I could learn from them. Others I just watched intently, learning from afar. You don't have to have regular lunch meetings with someone for them to mentor you.

If you pay attention, you can glean so many valuable lessons just from observation. I am always watching those who are excellent at what they do, learning from them how to improve myself. The inverse is also true. My mom once told me that if I would pay attention to my older sister's experiences and mistakes, and learn from them, there would be some struggles I could avoid.

Submitting to wisdom from God and from others is key to forward motion and growth—and success and purpose. We have to be teachable; we need a willingness to receive constructive criticism. It's the way we learn, improve, and grow. Actually, the only way we grow in the Lord is to be malleable in His hands. We must be willing to be corrected and reshaped by Him.

———

Hosting *Show Me St. Louis* at KSDK was a fun job, despite the steep learning curve. It took a couple of years, but I finally settled into my role and became confident in my work. It was, of course, not *all* sunshine and roses. I encountered a few colleagues who didn't seem to appreciate that a Miss America was hosting the show. And there were a couple of other people who were downright mean.

One particularly contentious interaction sent me to the ladies' room in tears. As I hid out in the restroom, feeling sorry for myself, another colleague walked in on my pity party. She asked me what was wrong. I told her about the argument that I'd just had with a coworker.

"Why doesn't she like me?" I whined.

"Who cares?" my friend Georgia replied. "You're the host, whether she or anyone else likes it. Unless you let her, she can't take that away from you. Now, dry your tears, hold up your head, and go out there and do your job. Don't give her this kind of power over your life!"

It was tough love but exactly what I needed. I wanted Georgia to coddle me and feel sorry for me. I wanted her to take my side. Instead, she told me to, in effect, grow up and stand tall in my position. Thank you, Georgia!

I worked through my first three-year contract with KSDK. I was hopeful that the station would offer me another contract. In other words, *not* fire me. Ultimately, they did offer me a contract renewal with a nice little raise. But the negotiations were tricky. My agent lobbied hard for favorable terms, but eventually hit a stalemate with my supervisor. So I asked for a meeting with my supervisor to see if I could help break the impasse. One of the terms that my agent wanted added to my new contract was what is known in the broadcast news business as a "network out." This simply means that if one of the national network news organizations (at that time, ABC, NBC, or CBS) offered me a job, then I could get out of the contract with my local station.

My supervisor didn't understand why I wanted this provision. To tell you the truth, I wasn't sure why Babette had pressed for it either. At that time, I had no designs on pursuing a network job. I was just riding this TV wave until it crested and petered out. But I trusted my agent and her wisdom, so I stood firm on the request.

"Debbye, I don't know why you want this network out," my supervisor said. "Your best chance for success is in local television." That was her not-so-veiled way of telling me that she didn't think I had any chance to make it in the "big time."

"Well, if that's the case, then there is no risk for you here," I quickly retorted.

She finally agreed to the provision. God was working and I didn't even know it. Two more years passed. I had a year remaining on my contract at KSDK and I was starting to get a little restless. It had been a fun job and I'd enjoyed most of my coworkers, but I sensed it was time to move on. Since I was still a fairly inexperienced journalist, I started looking for ways to hone my skills and prepare for the next step.

I decided to attend the National Association of Black Journalists' annual conference. My plan was to take a collection of my on-camera performances—a highlight reel—to the convention and ask the many attending television executives to critique my work. I just wanted to discover where and how I needed to improve for my budding journalism career to grow. I was not trying to find a job, and I did not have any expectations of being offered one. I just wanted to learn. I felt strongly that this was the right step for me to take.

While at the convention, Babette introduced me to Lyne Pitts. Lyne, at the time, was an executive producer of *The Early Show*, the national morning news program on CBS. I showed her my reel. She pulled no punches during her critique but gave me very valuable insight and advice. She was a pleasure. We had an engaging conversation.

As it ended, I offhandedly asked her if there were any job openings at *The Early Show*. I figured it couldn't hurt to ask.

She smiled and replied, "No, but I will keep you in mind if one becomes available." I took her response as a courteous brush-off. My feelings were not hurt. I figured she was being nice. I returned to St. Louis after the convention and didn't give my time there, or Lyne, another thought.

A few weeks later, Babette got a call from Lyne. A position was available and Lyne wanted me to come to New York City to interview for it. I could hardly believe my ears when Babette called me with the news. I took a couple of days off work at KSDK and flew to the Big Apple to see if there was a "bite" available for me. I met with Lyne again, as well as the senior executive producer and some of the senior producers. It happened so fast that I didn't have time to be nervous. I simply asked God to open the door if this was His will. I knew from experience that God can place you in the right place, with the right people, at the right time, if we just trust Him.

Before I knew it, the interviews were over, and I was on a plane back to St. Louis. By the time I landed, there was a message from Babette on my phone. I was offered the job. Thank God (and Babette) for the "network out" that we'd negotiated into my contract. I still had almost a year left on the contract. The only way I could accept the job was because of that provision. I gave my notice of resignation and started making plans to join *The Early Show* on CBS.

––––––––

If I thought working at KSDK in St. Louis was a wild ride, it was nothing compared to the demands of being a network reporter. Although initially I was a mere feature reporter, the expectations were high and the competition was fierce. I had to quickly learn how to pitch stories that would be approved by management to make it on the show. I had to learn to write better and faster. I had to improve my interviewing skills. Even though CBS was in third place in the morning TV ratings wars (behind NBC and ABC), this was the Tiffany Network, home of *60 Minutes*. I had to prove my worth every day.

At first, I reported periodic feature stories about life and lifestyle for a segment of the show called "Yikes! I'm a Grown Up." I shared this beat with another reporter, so my stories only made it on the show a couple of times a month. The prevailing sentiment in television is out-of-sight is out-of-mind. I knew that in order to have success at the network, I needed to be on the air more often.

To increase the number of my stories that aired, I offered to do pet stories. I told Steve Friedman, the senior executive producer, that people love their pets and that doing stories about pets and animals would be popular. He agreed, and a whole new niche for me was born. Soon I was doing weekly stories for a newly created segment called "Pet Planet." I became known as *The Early Show*'s resident veterinarian. Just like my first job out of veterinary school with Ralston Purina, this was tailor-made for me. It combined my knowledge and expertise in veterinary medicine with my developing skills as a network correspondent.

My job at CBS took me all over the country and occasionally around the world. I hit the million-mile club of air travel with one of the airlines. I was still doing speaking engagements when I could. Life just didn't slow down.

By 2003, I relocated to New York City and signed a second multiyear contract with CBS. In addition to animal-related stories, I covered human-interest stories and some breaking news. I snagged a one-on-one interview with President George W. Bush while he was in office. The story was about the "First Pets." That was an awesome experience.

President Bush was quite friendly and talkative. I was only given five minutes to interview him in the portico just outside the Oval Office. After I'd used up my time and asked all my questions, President Bush began to ask me questions. We'd exceeded our allotted time and the president's communications officer was turning purple with fury. But who was I to interrupt the president of the United States?

We stood there and chatted for several minutes. Finally, the president said goodbye. I thanked him for his time and virtually skipped back to the White House press briefing room where I would begin to write my story. I never got another one-on-one interview with a POTUS, but I didn't care. That one opportunity was worth the stern reprimand that I got from the communications officer for going over the time limit.

Over the course of the eleven years I was at CBS, I also reported for the *CBS Evening News*, *CBS Sunday Morning*, and hosted a prime-time television magazine program called *48 Hours on WE*. During that time, I also had a stint as an expert contributor on the show *DOGS 101* on Animal Planet. And I got to sideline report and cohost the Westminster Dog Show. I grew tremendously as a professional and a person. (Plus, I got married, but more about that in the next chapter!)

Never in my wildest childhood dreams did I ever think that I would spend more than a decade on network television. It was a challenging, exhilarating, and somewhat unstable experience. During my time at CBS, there were three executive leadership changes, four anchor team changes, and countless changes at the head of *The Early Show*. Each time one of these shifts happened, I would pray for God's favor and hope that I would survive the changes. Amazingly, I did . . . until 2011.

CBS News named a new president who decided to completely scrap *The Early Show* and rebuild it from the ground up. I was notified that my position would not be replicated at the new show, renamed *CBS This Morning*. I was told that although there wasn't a job for me on the morning show, I was well liked, and could perhaps find another place within the news division. I was flattered by the consideration.

I prayed to God to open a door if He wanted me to stay at CBS. But I sensed my season there was over. I no longer had a passion for what I was doing. So I asked the Lord to open the doors that He had for me and close the doors that weren't for me. I walked daily in the faith that God would direct my footsteps.

This was a very awkward time. All the attention and re-sources were directed toward launching the new morning show, so there was really no role for me. I still had a few months on my contract, so I showed up to work every day, dressed and camera-ready. I scoured newspapers, websites, and magazines for story ideas. I pitched a few here and there, but no one was interested. At the end of each day, I packed up my laptop and walked out the front door virtually un-noticed. I suppose I could have stopped showing up. I could have simply collected a paycheck until my contract expired. But I'm not built like that. I at least wanted to be present, just in case.

Although the CBS News leadership had offered to make room for me somewhere else in the news division, it became obvious that no real effort was being made to keep me. And, frankly, I was ready to go. During my time at CBS, I had tried several times to rise to an anchor position. I had many oppor-tunities to fill-in anchor when someone was away. But I never got a real shot to be a permanent anchor. I slowly began mov-ing my belongings out of my office. As the clock was running out on my contract at CBS, I decided to walk away and try to find an anchor job at another network or even on a local news station. I was not getting any younger, so if I was going to go for this advancement, now was the time.

On the last day of my contract, I came to work, packed up what was left in my office, turned in my company-issued electronics, and walked out the front door. There was no party, no goodbye salute, no thank you for eleven years. All eyes were on the new team and the new show. I'd become a part of the CBS past. I went home and cried. Not as hard as I'd cried after that third failed attempt at Miss Arkansas, but the defeat felt similar. I was embarrassed and hurt. A non-renewed contract in the news business is essentially a termination. I was uncertain about my future.

God, what do you want me to do now? I prayed.

I scheduled meeting after meeting with executives at the other networks, and even those at the New York local stations. I wasn't ready to leave television. I wanted to anchor. I had made up my mind that I wouldn't accept anything less. I was offered reporting jobs but no anchor positions. I stood my ground and held onto my faith.

My last day at CBS was February 18, 2012. For six months, I was unemployed. As the months ticked by, I began to get antsy. I had a little financial reserve, but it was dwindling quickly. I needed a job, sooner rather than later. And I was drained from the stress of job searching. I decided to keep trusting God to work things out. I had been doing my part, networking, going on interviews, having lunch and coffee meetings. Now I waited on Him to do what only He could do.

Two days into a much-needed vacation, I got a text message from my old boss and treasured friend, Lyne Pitts. It read, "Do you have time to talk about a job interview?" Lounging in a hammock when I read the message, I fell out of it trying to sit up. I replied, "Yes!" During our call, she told me that a new cable network was being formed, and the owner was looking for an anchor. He was in New York at that moment and was interested in meeting with me. That was the end of our vacation. My husband and I packed our bags, got on the next ferry back to the mainland, and drove through the night so I could meet with him.

I didn't know much about the owner or even what kind of operation the network would be, but I knew I wanted to anchor. I was game for the new adventure. Apparently, the interview went well. He offered me the job on the spot.

In the car on the drive home after the interview, I shouted and cried and praised God all the way home. It had been six months since I left CBS. I needed a job. Our reserve was running out. God moved just in the nick of time, as only He can do.

My first assignment was attending the World Economic Forum in Davos, Switzerland. What a way to start a new gig! Some of the wealthiest, most powerful, and most successful businesspeople and political leaders attend this annual confab in the Swiss Alps. I went from Davos to London, as the network's first bureau was there. Because the US operation hadn't started yet, I was asked to launch the network in London. For six weeks, I coanchored a nightly news show, occasionally flying home on weekends to see my family. It was simultaneously exhilarating and exhausting. But it was an answer to my prayers.

In the spring of 2013, the US bureau was finally ready to launch. I moved back home to a more stable schedule in what I thought at the time was a dream job. I had my own show where I delivered the news of the day and interviewed newsmakers and experts about a variety of issues. The team that worked on my show was small, so the work was hard and the days were long. But we loved what we were doing. The show aimed to feature stories about underserved people and communities, covering important stories that the major networks tended to ignore. I was proud of our efforts.

However, under even the best of circumstances a start-up company can be unstable, even volatile. That would be an understatement for this company. Paychecks were late, and eventually stopped coming altogether. This caused an extreme amount of distress for all the company employees. After three years of this financial roller coaster, I needed something reliable.

I prayed, now asking God for another job. By faith, I resigned from my position, believing God would again make a way. I knew that this company was no longer the place for me, but fear of being unemployed had kept me in that job for much longer than I should have stayed.

I resolved now that I would not make decisions based on my fears.

This was an important spiritual lesson for me to learn. It's important for you as well as you seek God's divine purpose. Making decisions based upon fear of the unknown is never a good decision-making strategy.

Fear is never a part of God's tactics. The Bible tells us, "For God has not given us a spirit of fear, but of power and of love and of a sound mind" (2 Timothy 1:7 NKJV). God does not use fear to accomplish His will and purpose. Fear is anti-faith. We should never make decisions out of feelings of fear and doubt; instead, we must let go of fear. We must intentionally choose to live by faith.

Faith is a decision, not a feeling. We may feel apprehensive, but we don't have to make decisions based on those feelings. We can decide to trust God no matter what the circumstances look like, knowing He will direct us. He promises, "Trust in the LORD with all your heart, and lean not on your own understanding; in all your ways acknowledge Him, and He shall direct your paths" (Proverbs 3:5–6 NKJV).

The very essence of faith is eager expectation. Waiting on the Lord should not be passive. We are not sitting down idly, waiting on some heavenly package to drop on our doorstep.

Usually, when we are eager for something, we prepare for it. When we believe in God's ability, we actively prepare for His performance. Are you believing God to provide the resources for law school? Then start studying for the Law School Admission Test, so when the opportunity arises, you'll be ready. Do you want to be a real estate mogul? Start studying for your real estate license. Do you want to be a chef? Start taking cooking classes at your local community center or YMCA. Don't despise small beginnings. Just start where you are. God will take it from there.

I started the tedious task of job hunting again. It was disheartening. Nothing seemed to open for me. Of course, I committed my job search and our finances to prayer. In a time of Bible study, I read 1 Kings 17, which tells of when God warned King Ahab, through the prophet Elijah, that there would be a drought in the land. God told Elijah to go to the Brook of Cherith, which would be a water source for Elijah during the drought.

God promised to feed Elijah there by sending a raven to deliver food every morning and every evening. After a time, the Brook of Cherith dried up. So God told Elijah to go to Zarephath where a Sidonian widow would provide food for him. Because Elijah obeyed God's commands, his needs were met without fail during the drought and related famine. One of the lessons from this story is that when we go through times of scarcity and lack, God will send us to a place where His provision resides.

As I waited in faith for a new job, the story spoke to me. It was as though God sent me to the new network when the CBS position "dried up." God provided abundantly there, but eventually that place "dried up" too. So I began to pray, "God send me to the next place of provision for me and my family." I didn't know what the source of my next job was, but I trusted God to lead me in the right direction.

A few weeks after I left my anchor position, I was talking on the phone with one of my closest friends, Dr. Jeanne Porter King. She is a consultant, coach, and trainer in leadership development. She runs her own very successful consulting business. As we were talking, I felt compelled to say to her, "Jeanne, if you ever need another trainer to help you with your clients, I would love to learn a new skill."

I should not have been surprised when she replied that, in fact, a client of hers required multiple trainers around the country to handle a project. She agreed to train me in her curriculum and assign me to some of the client's workshops. Jeanne was my Sidonian widow. In a time of professional drought, God worked through her to meet my needs.

I loved the work. It combined all the skills that I'd developed over the years: public speaking, teaching, and interpersonal relationship skills.

At Jeanne's encouragement, I created my own leadership curriculum in communications. I'd learned a lot as a Miss America, a motivational speaker, and a broadcast journalist. As if Jeanne had not done enough, she also introduced me to one of her clients. A whole new career was born. My consulting business remains young and growing. But already I have had the opportunity to train business and corporate leaders across the United States, as well as in Belgium, Scotland, and England. God continues to blow my mind with His awesome grace and favor.

Again, God may have multiple purposes for your life. He may have a number of opportunities for your work, employment, and personal interests. If you are open to His voice, the results will astound you.

An unlikely little girl from Arkansas grew up and became Miss America. Then she traveled the world as a motivational speaker. Then she enjoyed more than two decades in broadcast news. Now she has embarked on a new adventure as a consultant and trainer. Only God could have done these amazing things in my life. The apostle Paul said it so well, "Now to Him who is able to do exceedingly abundantly above all that we ask or think, according to the power that works in us, to Him be glory" (Ephesians 3:20 NKJV). To God be all the glory!

EIGHT

Patience

Being impatient is many people's Achilles' heel and a life-long weakness. Allow life's challenges to develop patience in you.

In terms of life accomplishments and milestones, mine have all taken time. I have had to learn to wait patiently. Still, being patient is not my favorite thing to do.

At times, my instincts are to push ahead, fight through the roadblocks, pull myself up off the floor, and keep going.

But sometimes God wants us to wait. His timing is important for our greater benefit in the long run. Sometimes He uses a waiting period to mature us, help us deepen our faith and grow, and bring us closer to Him.

Sometimes we need to wait in order to rest, to replenish. This brings to mind the Bible verse, "But those who wait on the Lord shall renew their strength; they shall mount up with wings like eagles, they shall run and not be weary, they shall walk and not faint" (Isaiah 40:31 NKJV).

In waiting, by developing patience, by being content in the moment, we align ourselves with God's divine timing.

But it still isn't my favorite thing to do.

"Why aren't *you* married?"

I was asked that question more than any other question while in my late twenties and thirties. And although I sometimes felt like people really meant to ask, "What's wrong with you?" I always politely responded, "I am waiting on God." But what I really wanted to yell at the top of my lungs, was, "I don't know. But I am happy just the way I am. Now leave me alone!"

But the real truth was, I was not content with being single. I wanted to be married . . . desperately.

That desperation did not define my life. Most days, I thrived and thought little of being single because my professional life, personal interests, and friends and family kept me busy *and* fulfilled. Other days, however, I experienced the loneliness that sometimes accompanies being unmarried.

> Who do you turn to in confidence when your patience is stretched thin?
>
> How could having an accountability partner strengthen your resolve to wait on God's time?
>
> By refocusing from "waiting is hard" to "waiting on God," how might you renew your strength?

Sometime in the late 1990s, I went on a cruise with the Turner side of my family. We'd decided to have our reunion on the high seas. It was my first cruise and I had a great time. Mostly.

About two days into the cruise, I noticed something depressing. Everywhere I looked, people in our party were in pairs. I was the only person alone. I became acutely aware of being single, and I didn't like it at all.

Once, after gorging at the midnight buffet, all the couples

went their separate ways on the ship. I was left staring out into the sky by myself on a deck. I looked down at the roiling ocean below and had a frightening thought: *If I fell overboard, how long would it take before someone would notice I'm missing?* Since there was no one on the ship who was specifically partnered with me, I wondered if it would take hours . . . or days. My thoughts shook me.

I was in my late twenties and, for the first time in my life, I felt utterly alone. I left the cruise more profoundly aware of my singleness. From then on, I also began to notice society is designed for couples and families. It's not always easy to be a single adult in today's culture. There are no tables set for one at restaurants. At some, you're forced to sit at the bar. There are no roller-coaster cars built for one; you have to ride alone or with a stranger.

The more I noticed such things, the more I became irritated at the way society operates. And the more I longed to be married. As I worked myself up into an I-don't-want-to-be-single-anymore frenzy, I even developed resentment toward the married couple who were leading the singles ministry at my church. Abstinence until marriage is commanded in the Bible, and my church encouraged the same. I thought that it was very easy for a married person to tell a single person to remain abstinent until marriage when a wife and husband could have sex whenever they wanted. My prevailing thought back then? *Walk a mile in my shoes, Buster!*

I want to be very clear: there is absolutely nothing wrong with being single. Singleness is not a sickness to be cured or a plague that threatens the very fabric of our culture, as some people think. I understand the desire to find a mate. I also came to understand the importance of living a full life *while* single.

I am thankful that God gave me the grace to be single and abstinent. But it wasn't always easy.

As a little girl I had imagined my family. I spent hours considering what my family life would be like. I made up scenarios and imagined our conversations. I drew pictures of the perfect family, or at least my vision of one. It included two boys, two girls, a dog, a cat, and a Volvo station wagon.

My husband would be kind and handsome, loving and protective. My children would be beautiful. I can remember coming up with names for them: Morgan, Noah, Trevor, and Taylor. They would be the perfect children with bright smiles and shiny faces and matching outfits. My pets would be well-behaved. My world would be complete with this idyllic clan. The truth is that I wanted the life depicted on the television show *The Brady Bunch*. Living the life of Carol Brady seemed like a dream come true.

I longed to be a part of that happy, loving, wealthy Brady family. In fact, as I've mentioned before, I loved family-oriented TV shows. I could not get enough of *Family Matters, Eight Is Enough,* and *The Partridge Family* because they were foreign to me. I grew up in a single-parent home with a very busy working mother and an older sister who didn't particularly want to be bothered with me. The lifestyle I saw portrayed on those shows seemed picture-perfect. And I wanted it badly.

My playtime with friends also reflected my desire for marriage and a perfect family. We would always fight over who got to be married to Demond Wilson, the actor who played Lamont on the TV show *Sanford and Son*. He was hot stuff back in those days. We would imagine that we were in church or going shopping or out to dinner and act out our parts as wife and mother with our celebrity husbands and brood of children. That was my absolute favorite game.

But as I got older, I began to notice a disturbing trend among my mother's friends: marriage was the sole goal of many single women. As I've shared before, my mom was a counselor by profession. She had a degree in Sociology and Rehabilitation Counseling, and was also a Bible teacher and spiritual mentor. Very often, people from our community (mostly young women) called or visited my mom to get advice and prayer about some problem. More often than not, the women were single—and distraught about it. Single woman after single woman begged, "Sister Turner, please pray that God will send me a husband. I *need* a husband." My mother always advised them to wait on God, trust in the Lord, and be about God's work at this stage in their lives.

I was never allowed to be in the room when my mother had these counseling and prayer sessions, but I often hid around the corner and listened to their conversations. They were fascinating and mysterious. They also seemed desperate and needy. I remember thinking, *These women are pathetic! I don't ever want to be like that.*

Based on the conversations I overheard, I prayed, "God please help me to always be content with You. Don't ever let me feel like I have to have a husband in order to be happy." I deeply wanted to be married one day, but I didn't want to lose my dignity over it. I wanted to live a full, happy life and, when the right time and the right man came along, I wanted to know. I asked God to let me recognize him instantly. And I asked God to help me be satisfied as a single person until it was time for me to get married. God honored that prayer for contentment.

I went through my twenties focused on pursing my education, career, and ministry. When I won the Miss America pageant, my life went into warp speed, never slowing down through finishing veterinary school, and starting a career in broadcast news. All of that was God's answer to a little girl's prayer for contentment and happiness in Him.

I now understand that I can draw a straight line from the fact that I grew up in a single-parent home without my father to the fact that I remained single until my early forties. My parents separated when I was five years old and divorced not long after.

As the years went by, I began to understand what my father's absence from our home meant. No dad to fix the washing machine when it broke down. No dad to mow the lawn or shovel the snow. No dad to take me to the father-daughter school dance. No dad to carry me on his back or play tickle-monster. No dad to help me understand boys and their odd behavior.

As I entered adolescence, I made a firm decision. Although I liked boys, I made up my mind that I would never allow one to hurt me emotionally the way my father had hurt my mother. My mom never once dragged my sister or me into the gory details of her relationship with my dad. In fact, at the time, I had no clue why they divorced. But from time to time, I caught glimpses of the emotional pain my mom endured because of her failed marriage. Until the day she died, she pined for my father. She loved him intensely. And no one ever took his place in her life. I built emotional barriers to protect myself from that kind of disappointment and hurt. As a result, I did not trust easily, if at all. I was terrified that if I let someone get too close, he would reject me.

A fear of abandonment was the boogeyman in my emotional closet. Every choice I made about relationships and friendships was filtered through the simple question, "Will this person leave me?" So anytime a relationship got too intense, I would do something stupid to sabotage it. In my mind, it was better I left him before he had the chance to leave me. There was a time I was proud about the fact that not one of my boyfriends broke up with me; I was the breaker-upper. No surprise, then, that I remained single until forty-two.

I came close to marriage in college. I had started dating a smart, kind, popular, and handsome guy during my junior year in high school. We dated through the end of high school and remained together even when we both ended up going to different colleges. I attended Arkansas State University in Jonesboro. He went to pharmacy school out of state. He proposed before I was scheduled to leave Jonesboro to attend veterinary school in Missouri. We'd been together for five years and it seemed like the logical next step.

I said yes even though I had misgivings. My hesitation had nothing to do with his faults (we all have them) or doubts of my love for him. I loved him dearly. But I knew in my heart that we wanted different lives. I knew that his future was not my future. The life he was destined to lead was not the life that I believed I was destined to lead. I couldn't reconcile the difference. The bottom line: he was a good choice, but he was not God's choice for me.

Yet, I had accepted the proposal and ring anyway. I couldn't bear the thought of losing him. I couldn't bear the thought of hurting him by saying no. So we got engaged. As we began to talk about our future and the life we wanted together, I started working diligently to fit the proverbial square peg version of myself and my dreams into the round hole version of the ones we discussed. Our goals were that different.

The disconnect tortured me for a full year. The longer I let the engagement go on, the more I realized a long-term relationship would be a problem for us both. Either I would break up with him as we were planning a wedding, or I would enter a marriage that I wasn't totally convinced would work. Neither option was viable to me.

I finally worked up the courage to tell him how I felt. It was excruciating. It was hard to explain that I deeply loved him, but I didn't want to marry him. It didn't make sense. He had done nothing wrong. I was not in love with anyone else. I just knew that I wasn't the right person for him. And vice versa. Worse yet, he truly was my best friend. When we broke up, I lost my closest friend.

What a mess I had made. It took years to fix the damage. I am grateful today that my former fiancé found love again with the right person for him. I even attended his wedding.

———

In my twenties, I had very little time to think about being single. I was too busy. But when I hit my mid-thirties, suddenly my ovaries became very noisy. The imaginary ticking of my womb was deafening. My biological clock was about to strike midnight.

Being single in my thirties was tougher than when I was younger because of the vast number of people I knew who were in relationships. Holidays were always a challenge.

One year in the mid 1990s, Thanksgiving was approaching. Because I was single, I usually invited myself to the Thanksgiving festivities at one of my relatives' homes. That particular year, I decided that I would instead wait and see who would invite me over for Thanksgiving dinner. I just wanted to see who would remember to include me. Little did I know that I was setting myself up for disappointment.

As the weeks went by, no one asked me over. Not my friends. Not my sister. Not even my father. With only a week before Thanksgiving, I was distraught. *No one really loves me! No one really cares!* I started spiraling into depression. All the emotional decorations were in place for a full-blown pity party.

Then God spoke to my heart. He said, *Are you the only person on earth with no plans for Thanksgiving?*

I instantly thought of a dozen single women who probably didn't have anywhere to go on that day. Instead of feeling sorry for myself, pining for a blessing from God, I decided I would be a blessing *of* God. I invited coworkers and friends, whom I knew would not get to go home for the holiday, to my place for dinner. I cooked a huge meal. And we had a grand time. When the last guest left, I realized that I was not lonely or forlorn once all day. God taught me a critical lesson. As we reach out to others to bless them, we get blessed in the process.

The apostle Paul wrote, "For I have learned in whatever state I am, to be content" (Philippians 4:11 NKJV). This verse can easily be misinterpreted. Most think that *content* only means being happy, satisfied, or fulfilled. Actually, one definition is to "wait quietly." A person may not be happy with being single, but the key is to learn to wait quietly. Allow God to show you His purpose for your life. Be open to God's timing and seasons. Seek His face. Pursue His heart. Only God's love can fill the void in our life. Absolutely no one can complete us like He can.

I might challenge you in the same way I was challenged that Thanksgiving. In this time of waiting, what is God trying to teach you? What might you do with other people? How might you focus on God?

You see, waiting is not necessarily a time of inaction. There are things you can do. There are ways you can help others. There are new areas of knowledge or expression you can explore.

I don't believe God intends for us to do absolutely nothing while we are waiting on Him. Our lives go on. Don't let the waiting period immobilize you. Buy the house, start the business, launch the project. Fulfill your God-given purpose during this time of life. God does not waste our time. So *we* must not waste our time either.

Waiting upon the Lord doesn't mean you are prohibited from doing things. I believe God uses the actions we take in life to map out what He has for us in the future.

Other than being single, life was pretty great on the brink of forty. I was traveling the world as a correspondent for *CBS News* and doing motivational speaking. By this time, I'd also become an ordained reverend in my church. I preached, taught Bible studies, prayed for people. Life was good. While I longed for marriage, I began to believe it would not happen.

The statistics are discouraging for the likelihood of single women over forty ever getting married. The truth is, not everyone who wants to marry actually does. I began to think I was destined to be one of those people. So I resigned myself to the very real possibility of being single for the rest of my life.

I prayed and asked God to help me be OK with a lifetime of singleness. "God, if it is my destiny to remain single for the rest of my life, if that is your will for me, I accept it. But please take away the desire for marriage and a family. I am willing to be single. I just need that to be enough." After praying, I increasingly plunged into work and life's activities. I thought I could outrun the desire for marriage. If I were busy enough, then maybe I wouldn't have time to even think about it. I worked and I worked, but I couldn't stop wanting to be married. It wasn't long before I learned why.

I couldn't outrun marriage because marriage was God's plan for my life. It just didn't happen the way I intended it to happen.

In my late twenties and thirties, I had a friendship with a great guy. He loved God, was fun to be around, and was very supportive. We'd decided early in the relationship to be just friends. Neither of us were, at that point, ready for marriage. We agreed that we'd nurture a healthy friendship and if God led us into something more later, then great. I loved his family. They became my family.

Over the course of my friendship with this man, there had been times when he was ready to move forward in our relationship, and times when I wanted to move forward. But we were never in sync. When I finally decided that I wanted to get married and he seemed like the logical choice, he definitely was not interested in marrying me. Our friendship had hit a couple of bumps in the road. I later learned he was developing a "friendship" with another woman. I tried my best to win him back. I cried, prayed, begged God, and asked friends to pray. It just wasn't working out. After ten years, we ended our friendship. I was heartbroken.

What I didn't know at the time was that the person God intended for me to marry had been in my life the whole time. I just couldn't see him for who he was.

I met my future husband fifteen years before we got married. Yes, *fifteen years!*

In 1993, I was traveling full-time as a motivational speaker. At that time, Gerald Bell was a talent manager and event planner who booked me to be one of the speakers for a Christian youth rally in Columbus, Ohio. We met a few weeks before the rally to take publicity photographs, as I had a speaking engagement in Columbus. I have absolutely no memory of that meeting. I know it happened, because there is a photograph documenting the meeting. Otherwise, it was unremarkable for me.

I returned to Columbus for the youth rally, as planned. It apparently went well because I was invited back to Xenia, Ohio, the following year to speak at a church singles' retreat. The church sponsoring the retreat hired Gerald to book me for this event, since he'd contacted me for the youth rally the year before. It was Gerald's responsibility to get me to and from the airport. My first memory of him was having dinner with him after the retreat was over. I had some extra time before my flight departed, so we decided to stop and grab a bite to eat on the way to the airport.

I remember our time together very well. Gerald was just a nice guy. He was easy to talk to and fun to be around. What I liked most about Gerald that evening was his approach to me. He was not trying to flirt and "run game" on me. I didn't feel like I had to protect myself or my honor around him.

We had great conversation. We talked about our lives and dreams. We talked about how we felt God was working in our lives. We also talked about our desires for marriage. I told him that I had asked God to let me marry my best friend. In my estimation, I explained, a solid friendship would be a sound foundation for a long, happy marriage. Passion can fade over time. Healthy friendships grow stronger with time.

I didn't know at the time how earnestly Gerald took my statement regarding marrying my best friend. I also didn't have a so-called "love connection" with Gerald that evening. I was not attracted to him. There was no lightning bolt from heaven with God's voice declaring, "This is your husband!" Gerald was just a nice guy, and I liked him a lot. We exchanged phone numbers and agreed to stay in touch. I caught my flight and went on with my life. I really didn't give Gerald or our great conversation much thought.

As we had agreed, Gerald called me occasionally. I heard from him once, maybe twice, a year. We enjoyed more great conversation, even prayed together, then returned to our respective lives. At the time, he was no more than a brother in Christ. In fact, over the next several years as our friendship grew, we even discussed our separate dating relationships. We'd prayed with each other and consoled one another when those relationships didn't go well. Gerald had a front-row seat to the ten-year friendship I mentioned earlier. Because Gerald was just a friend, I felt no hesitation pouring out my broken heart about how things fell apart.

In the fall of 2000, during one of our annual phone calls, I shared with Gerald about my search for a new assistant, given that my current one was relocating out of state. I needed someone to help with booking and arranging the details of my speaking engagements. As I told him of my situation, it occurred to me that he was more than capable of providing the services I needed. I asked him if he would take me on as a client, booking and coordinating my appearances. He was hesitant.

"I don't want to jeopardize our friendship," he said.

I was perplexed by his reluctance. While we had become genuine friends, we only talked a couple times a year, at most. What was there to jeopardize? We discussed the job and his concerns. Gerald is a man of prayer, so I wasn't surprised when he finally said, "Let me pray about it. I'll give you an answer in a week."

As promised, he called a week later with his decision: he would become my booking manager. However, wanting to ensure our friendship would be preserved no matter what happened in our professional dealings, he'd drawn up a "friendship contract" detailing what could go wrong and how to address the issues. I thought the attention to detail was amusing. I signed the contract and was grateful to have him as a booking manager.

Looking back, I should have known that Gerald's feelings for me went beyond friendship, but I was oblivious.

Once Gerald started working with me, our interaction increased exponentially. We went from talking a couple of times a year to talking several times a week, discussing the details of my overloaded speaking and travel schedule. I came to really depend on him.

Yet, Gerald was still just a brother in Christ. I had no romantic feelings for him. In fact, I tried to set him up with my best friend. "Girl, he's a *good* man. This is the kind of man you want to marry!" I told her about him. Her immediate response was, "Then why aren't you dating him?" I shot back, "He's like a brother to me. I can't date my brother."

Gerald worked with me for about five years. Then, in 2005, he informed me that he'd been hired for a new job in Michigan and wouldn't be able to continue coordinating my speaking engagements. His new position would not leave time to also work with me. I was really sorry to learn that. I was happy about his career progress, but I'd come to depend on him as a friend and booking manager.

His last project for me was a speaking engagement in Minnesota at the American Veterinary Medical Association annual convention. Speaking at the event was a big deal that required a lot of logistical planning. I needed him there with me.

The speech went well. And, as usual, Gerald did his job superbly. I couldn't have pulled it off without him. When it was time for us to return to our respective homes, we went to the airport together.

That's when Gerald began to act strange. He started stuttering. "I have something that I need to tell you. I have avoided sharing this with you for many years, but I have to say something. I will regret it for the rest of my life if I don't tell you," he finally said. "I have loved you since the first day I met you."

What? I was shocked.

He explained how he'd been in love with me for years. He said that his other dating relationships didn't work out because he compared them to me, and they just weren't me. Gerald talked for quite some time about his feelings and hopes.

The whole time he was talking, all I could think was, *How do I let him down easy?*

While I was flattered by his transparency and sentiment, I just didn't like him like *that*. After he finished pouring out his heart, I took a deep breath and replied, "Thank you."

That's not really what you want to hear when you tell someone that you love them, right? I added, "While I do love you as a brother, I can't offer you the same kind of love that you are offering me."

Obviously, that was not what he was hoping to hear.

To his credit, he took it like a champ. He squared his shoulders and said, "No problem. I just had to try. Let's forget I said anything. Let's just go back to being friends."

I think sometimes during our waiting periods in life, God is telling us, "Go!" He is showing us a path forward. He is revealing His will to us.

And yet, even in our waiting frustration, our impatience and insistence on something happening, we say no to the answer God has placed right in front of us.

Yet even in our "nos" God says yes. Even when we can't recognize God's great plan for us, He is patient and keeps working His plan.

By the beginning of 2006, I realized that Gerald hadn't called me in a couple of months, so I called him. "Hey, stranger!" I said. "It's been a while since we've spoken. I didn't hear from you during Christmas. That's unusual. What's happening with you?" I wasn't mad at him. I just missed our friendship.

"Yes, I know I haven't called. I thought I could just be your friend, but I can't right now," he explained. "I want to one day find my wife and get married. I can't do that if I am still hung up on you. And I can't get over you if we are talking all the time. I need a season of silence. We'll be friends again one day. I just need some time."

His reply surprised me, but I understood completely. After all, I'd liked guys before who didn't like me back. I got it. I told him to take the time he needed and noted that I would be waiting to resume our friendship when he was ready.

I remember exactly where I was during that conversation: in my car on the way to teach a Bible study at my church. By the time we ended the phone call, I was taking the Linden Boulevard exit off the Van Wyck Freeway in Queens, New York. I recall the conversation and my location because the moment I hit the "end" button on my cell phone, my heart began to ache.

Immediately, I began to miss Gerald, knowing that he wouldn't be calling me anymore. I was surprised by the surge of emotion; I had not missed him like that during the previous two months when I hadn't heard from him.

Over the next few days, I couldn't get Gerald out of my thoughts. I decided to send him an email just to say "hello." I didn't want to call because he'd been clear that we shouldn't talk for a while. In the email, I wrote that I missed our friendship and looked forward to the day we could resume communication. Oddly, he did not reply to my email. As time passed, I began to get annoyed. *How could he ignore me?*

A couple of weeks later, I decided to call his cell phone at a time that I knew he wouldn't answer so I could leave a voicemail message. He was scheduled to run a marathon the coming weekend, so that was my pretext for the call. I left a message wishing him a good run in the marathon, and told him again that I missed him. I thought for sure he would call me back. I wanted to hear his voice.

Days went by and there was no return call. I think I emailed him one last time, asking him to reply just so I would know that he was OK. Nothing. Crickets.

When I bemoaned his silence to my dear friend Jeanne, she replied, "Well, Debbye, if he is just a friend, then why do you care so much?"

That set off bells in my spirit. It was a life-changing question. *Why did I care so much?* I think I muttered something to her about common decency and courtesy, but the truth was I had to face the real answer. The trouble was, at that moment, I didn't know it. I wasn't ready to fully accept the truth yet.

I stopped trying to reach Gerald and started reaching out to God. I began to pray, "OK, God, who is this man? Why can't I get him out of my mind? What is Your purpose here?"

Strangely, instead of providing some great revelation about Gerald, God began to show me the broken places *in my heart.* Over the next few months, as I prayed, I also journaled. As I wrote out my prayers and feelings, a pattern emerged.

God showed me how I had avoided true intimacy in any relationship or friendship because of my fear of being hurt. I was afraid to let people get too close to my heart because I feared being rejected. This fear of rejection stemmed from the emotional pain that I saw my mother experience after my parents' divorce. I thought if people got to *really* know me, they would not like me. So I taught myself to wear a mask of confidence and charisma. But I kept everyone at arm's length.

Ironically, I also was afraid of being abandoned. During this time of prayer and revelation, I realized my fear stemmed from how I perceived my father had rejected my mother and abandoned us. I never got over him leaving our home. I realized I was not as cavalier at five years old as I thought I'd been. I was concerned with more than getting pizza for dinner. Throughout my childhood, when events that required the presence of my absent father came and went—school concerts, prom, and more—I felt abandoned. *Why isn't my father here to take me to the father-daughter dance at school? Why isn't my dad here to lecture my boyfriends on getting me home in time for curfew?*

I buried these feelings. I declared that I didn't need my dad. I defiantly told people that my single-parent home was not a "broken home." And while my mom worked tirelessly to give her two daughters the best possible life, the one thing she couldn't give us was our father. I had spent my whole life believing my parents' divorce had no effect on me. But as I prayed for wisdom regarding Gerald and worked through feelings of abandonment, I was coming to realize that wasn't true. The hurt, fear, and insecurities sparked from my parents' divorce had seeped into my every decision.

With God's help, I spent the summer of 2006 confronting my emotional baggage.

I prayed and asked God to heal my heart. I journaled and admitted my real feelings. I talked through those feelings with a trusted friend. It was like peeling the layers of an onion. With each layer removed, I could more clearly see myself and the world around me. This was hard work—not particularly fun, but necessary for me to be free and able to maintain healthy relationships. By the end of the summer, I felt like a different person—newer and lighter.

In this new freer state, I also had an epiphany. Everything concerning character and integrity that I had asked God for in a husband, Gerald had. Granted, he didn't have the portfolio of material possessions or even the physical characteristics I thought I had wanted, but he was the *kind* of man I longed for. We'd been friends for thirteen years—how had I missed realizing this before?

It was a bittersweet revelation. Sweet because God had given me a breakthrough into understanding my heart and emotions. Bitter because I hadn't heard from Gerald in almost a year. He was still in his "season of silence." I wasn't sure if we'd ever talk again. I had given up trying to reach him.

He clearly didn't want to talk to me. Yet, there I was: healed, transformed, and in love with a guy who wouldn't talk to me.

I thought I'd missed my opportunity with Gerald. The best I could hope for was that God would send someone else, at some point. All I could do was move on with life. Determined to do so, I gave the whole matter to God. I told Him, "I missed it. You sent my husband to me and I was too messed up and proud to recognize him. I am so sorry. Please send someone else."

Waiting seasons serve different purposes. It may be that a time of waiting exists for you to wrestle with unresolved issues. God may have set aside time in your life for you to sort through your emotional baggage—alone or with help from a mental health professional.

> Are there struggles you have in your life right now that are holding you back?
>
> What is God whispering to you about them?
>
> If you are in a season of waiting, how can you use it to unpack any emotional baggage?

Weeks after I'd asked God to send someone else, in the wee hours of September 15, 2006, an email popped into my inbox. My heart skipped a beat when I saw the return email address—it was from Gerald. It had been more than a year since our fateful conversation at the Minneapolis–St. Paul airport, and nine months since our last phone conversation when he declared this "season of silence." (Yes, I was counting!)

But it was a blast email sent to a long list of people. He stated that his mother was gravely ill and asked for prayer. I was grateful he'd included me on the list, and I immediately replied I was so sorry to learn of his mom's condition, would definitely be praying, and noted I was sorry I had not been in his life to support him through that difficult time. I concluded, "Remember, you still have a friend in New Jersey." I hoped he would read between the lines and understand I wanted our friendship to resume whenever he was ready.

Gerald called me later that day, informing me his mother had passed away. I was so sorry. I asked him if I could attend her funeral, promising I wouldn't bother him. I just wanted to be there in case he needed me. He consented to my attendance, and a couple of days later, he called again asking if I would read a Scripture and pray during her service. Of course, I said yes.

I flew to Columbus, Ohio, to attend Gerald's mom's funeral. I was excited to see him, but also nervous. I didn't know how we would react to each other. And he didn't know I was now in love with him. I wasn't sure what to do with my surging emotions. When I arrived at the church for the wake, which was immediately before the service, I scanned the people in the sanctuary, looking for Gerald. There were a lot of people there. Julia Bell, Gerald's mom, was highly regarded in the community.

There was a crowd of people in the front, near the pulpit. I figured Gerald must be in that crowd, so I headed down the center aisle toward the front of the sanctuary. I just wanted to say hello and let him know I was there.

"There's Miss America." "That's Debbye Turner." I could hear people talking as I passed them. I was still recognizable as Miss America 1990, plus at the time I was on national television as a correspondent for CBS News.

As I approached the crowd of people who were gathered in the front, it was like a scene from a movie. The people stepped aside to let me through, like the parting of the Red Sea. I didn't have to say, "Excuse me," people just stepped out of my way.

Sure enough, at the center of this crowd of people stood Gerald.

I was struck by how different he looked from the last time we'd seen each other. He looked taller. He was thinner. He looked confident. He looked . . . gorgeous.

He no longer looked like *just* a nice guy. He didn't look like my brother in Christ. He looked like a man, a delicious man.

Most of all, he looked like my husband.

I can't explain it completely, but I knew in my spirit that Gerald was my husband. I was definitely attracted to him, but it went deeper than that. I remembered the prayer I prayed as a little girl asking God to let me recognize my husband the instant I met him. I wasn't just meeting Gerald. We'd met fifteen years earlier. But in that moment, my world shifted. Something was different. I was different. And I recognized my husband: Gerald.

But certainly Mrs. Bell's funeral was not an appropriate place to declare my love to her grieving son.

He finally looked up from a conversation and saw me. "You made it. Thank you for coming," he said warmly. We hugged. I expressed my condolences, and told him I was honored to be there, then stepped aside so other people could talk to him.

I hate to admit it, but during Mrs. Bell's entire funeral, I couldn't help thinking about her son. And I couldn't take my eyes off of him.

Along with leading prayer during the service, I confess I silently prayed that Gerald wasn't dating anyone. I prayed it wasn't too late for us.

After the service, I attended the repast where friends and relatives gathered to eat and reminisce. Afterward, when Gerald was seated alone on his mom's piano bench, I slid next to him and asked him to catch me up on what was happening in his life. How was his new job in Michigan going? What else was happening in his life?

As he began to recount his life to me, I again prayed, "God, please don't let him be dating anyone."

After telling me about his job, his pursuit of a master's degree in communications, his next marathon, his church, he finally said, "Oh, and I am dating someone."

Forcing a smile, I replied, "That's wonderful. Tell me about her." But on the inside, I was screaming, *Noooooooo!* I listened politely as he told me about his new girlfriend. With each piece of information, my heart broke a little more.

I really had missed my opportunity with Gerald.

At the funeral, Gerald mentioned he was running the Chicago marathon. I was a runner too and had run in a number of marathons. It happened that I was slated to run the Chicago marathon too. We agreed to meet up there, and even start the race together.

For me, that held mixed emotions.

When the day of the marathon arrived, I was excited to see Gerald, but I dreaded it too. I didn't know how I would react to seeing him again, and I wasn't sure I could keep my strong emotions for him in check. We met at McCormick Place, the convention center in Chicago, to pick up our runners' packet. As we strolled the aisles of the marathon expo, I yearned for him to know how I really felt. I couldn't bring myself to say anything.

When it was time to leave, Gerald headed for one set of doors to meet up with his friend. As he walked away from me, I had this overwhelming sense that my future was slipping away. It felt like the life God had for me was walking out the door with Gerald. Panicked, I shouted, "Gerry!" (Gerry is his childhood nickname and the name I call him.) He turned back to look at me. I didn't know exactly what to say.

"If things don't work out with your girlfriend, we should talk again," I blurted out. That was it. That was the best I could come up with.

His eyebrows raised a bit and he replied, "OK. I'll call you."

It was a little bit of hope. That was all I needed. "He is going to call me," I repeated to myself as I walked toward the entrance where my friend was waiting. In my imagination, Gerald was going to go back to Michigan after the marathon and break up with his girlfriend. I figured he would need a few days to recoup from the breakup, then he'd call me.

The next morning, we found each other and started the marathon together. I knew he would eventually pull ahead of me because he was a faster runner. But I made the most of the time we ran together. I laughed, flirted, and batted my eyes. I'm sure I looked ridiculous. I didn't care. I hoped that he would come back to me.

When the marathon was over, and it was time to leave, we hugged a final time. He said, "I'll talk to you soon." I did a little twirl in my head, but calmly responded, "OK. Sounds good."

I flew back to New Jersey and waited for the call. When a week passed and I hadn't heard from him, I didn't worry. I figured the breakup was more complicated than I'd imagined. Another week passed; then a month went by. The year came to an end, and still no call from Gerald. I figured that maybe things did work out with his girlfriend; maybe he decided to stay in the relationship. I resigned myself to the fact that I messed this one up.

I started dating someone else.

He was intriguing, but he wasn't Gerald.

———

Maybe you're in a waiting place in which you feel you've missed God's timing, that a great opportunity has now passed you by. Maybe you too have said to God, with tears in your eyes, "Please send someone else," or "Please provide me another opportunity," but secretly wonder if you missed out.

Well, I believe God works things together for good.

And I believe He is more than capable of providing us the desires of our heart.

After all, He is God. He can work things out in our favor.

In January of 2007, I got a New Year's greeting card from Gerald. The message was something pretty standard like "Wishing you a blessed and prosperous New Year." Nothing remarkable about it. But, in the fifteen years I'd known Gerald, he'd never sent me a New Year's card. I figured something was up, but I didn't know what. I texted him to acknowledge receiving the card and wished him a Happy New Year.

Then he called me. He said that he had something to tell me but he wanted to do it in person, if possible. Oh no. I figured this news could only be that he was going to marry his girlfriend. *Shoot. Shoot. Shoot.* We compared our schedules, looking for a window of time to see each other. I was booked full with travel commitments for CBS and he with his work travel. After a couple of days of texting possible dates (and cities) to meet each other, he finally said, "Never mind. We can just talk on the phone. I will call you this Saturday."

He called at the precise time he'd said he would. There were very few pleasantries. "I'm going to get right to it," Gerald said. I braced myself.

"I've been on a sixty-day consecration, praying about God's direction and purpose for my life," he announced. *Oh lawd, here it comes*, I thought.

Then, my whole world changed.

"I can't get you out of my spirit, Debbye. I feel called to you. I feel like my purpose is to help you fulfill God's purpose in your life."

I think I stopped breathing.

He went on, "I don't know if I am out on this limb by my-self again, but I thought I would try one last time." My heart was bursting. I began to cry quietly. This seemed impossible. Five minutes before, I thought he was going to tell me that he was marrying someone else.

Taking a deep breath, I managed to say, "You're not on that limb by yourself." I opened up and told him about the journey of healing and restoration that I'd gone through the previous summer. I told him how I felt when I saw him at his mother's funeral and at the Chicago marathon.

In that moment, we both exhaled.

Two weeks later we met at the Brooklyn Diner on West 57th Street in Manhattan, just down the block from Carnegie Hall. It had been hard to coordinate our schedules. This was the time that worked out, and Gerald offered to fly to New York.

I wasted no time in announcing to Gerald, "I don't need to date you. I've known you for fifteen years. I know who you are. I believe we are at this juncture by God's design, so let's not waste time. Ask me any question you have for me. I think you'll like the answer."

Yes, I actually said that. I'm mortified by my presumptuous, bold words now but at the time I was dead serious. *Remember, I admitted that waiting isn't my favorite thing to do.*

Gerald blinked a couple of times, then held up his hands. "Wait, wait, wait. Let's just slow down a minute," he said. "Yes, we've known each other a long time. But we have not known each other in a dating relationship. This is the most important decision we will make in our lives. Let's not skip any steps. Let's date." Gerald's suggestion was not what I wanted to hear, but it made sense. We mapped out a schedule for seeing each other, since we lived in different cities. Basically, we planned to see each other every other weekend. We would alternate who would fly to whom. We started talking daily on the phone, several times a day. It was wonderful. I was dating my best friend. What could be better?

Being married?

Yes, I was very anxious to get married. I wanted to start a family. I also wanted to book a great venue for our wedding. In New York City, the best venues go fast and are booked, sometimes, years in advance. I refused to put a deposit on a wedding venue until I had a ring on my finger. A girl has standards.

Gerald seemed to be in no hurry. As the months went by, I started to get irritated. What was taking him so long to propose? In the meantime, as we embarked on this journey toward knowing each other in this new and different way, it became clear that we both still had emotional baggage that could potentially harm our relationship. Even though I had grown tremendously in the previous year, I still had fears and hang-ups as a result of previous failed relationships. Gerald and I agreed we wanted to have a healthy, strong, lifelong marriage and did not want to drag emotional baggage from childhood or previous relationships into our relationship. That wouldn't be fair or smart.

So we decided to get counseling, *individually*. It was important for each of us to face and resolve our individual emotional issues before being ready to move forward in a marriage together.

This was the best decision we ever made.

Even though we were going through this wonderful process in counseling, I was growing ever more impatient. Gerald and I had been dating for seven or eight months, and he still hadn't proposed. I really wanted to book that wedding venue, which meant I needed an engagement ring. It sounds so silly and superficial now, but at the time it was a real crisis in my mind.

My family invited Gerald to spend Thanksgiving with us at a rented beach house on North Carolina's Outer Banks. *This was perfect*, I thought. He would surely propose in front of my family. My sister, cousins, and I began to speculate about whether it would happen. I worked myself up into a frenzy for no reason.

He didn't propose.

So surely it will be Christmas, I thought. We'd planned to spend time together between Christmas and the New Year. But no proposal. Not even on New Year's Eve. I was beyond frustrated; I was annoyed. I finally demanded to know when he was going to propose. I couldn't understand what was taking so long. We were sitting at the Grand Rapids airport waiting for my flight back to New York. I was crestfallen I was not engaged. On my last day at work before leaving for the holiday, I'd giddily announced to my coworkers, "I'm getting engaged! When I come back from my time off, I'll have a ring on my finger!" I even got a manicure to make sure my hands looked their best for this big moment.

I admitted to Gerald that I had bragged to my friends that I was getting engaged during the holiday. I whined that I didn't understand what was taking him so long. I asked him if he was having second thoughts.

Gerald said, "I got this, Debbye, just trust me. You don't have to be in control of everything. Trust me." I felt a little better, but I was still going home with a naked finger. I tried to put engagement out of my mind. I figured he'd probably propose on Valentine's Day.

I know. I was pathetic.

Our next scheduled visit was the weekend of January 11, 2008. It was our normal visit. Not a special day or holiday. We had a lovely time.

On Sunday, before his flight home, we had a little extra time, so Gerald suggested that we do something touristy. There were several New York landmarks he hadn't visited so he wanted to sightsee a little. He chose the Empire State Building, a choice I wasn't particularly enthusiastic about because of the weather. The observation deck of the Empire State Building is outside, windy, and more than one thousand feet in the air. It would be freezing up there. But I agreed.

As we looked out at the marvelous vistas of New York City and the surrounding areas from the Empire State Building, I served as a tour guide to Gerald. From each side of the observation deck, I pointed out notable buildings, parks, neighborhoods, and landmarks. I did this mainly to distract myself from how cold I was and to help the time go by faster. We completed our walk around all four sides of the observation deck, then went inside to the gift shop to warm up.

I was ready to leave but Gerald said, "Before we go, let's walk around the observation deck one more time." I reluctantly agreed and we ventured back out into the cold and wind.

This time, as we circled the deck, I quizzed Gerald on the landmarks that I'd previously pointed out. Again, I did this just to keep my mind occupied while my fingers and toes fought frostbite. Mercifully, we finally finished our second tour.

Gerald said, "OK, I passed your test. Now it's my turn to ask the questions." I was looking out at the city. When I turned to look at him, Gerald was kneeling. At first, I wasn't sure what was happening. Did he drop something? Was he tying his shoe? His next words made it abundantly clear.

"Debbye Turner, I love you with all my heart," I heard him say.

Then my mind started racing. *Oh my. Oh my. He's proposing! How do my nails look?* Gerald continued saying the most wonderful sentiments, much of which I barely remember because I was waiting on him to stop talking so I could say,

"Yes!" He finally ended his romantic soliloquy with, "I am so grateful that God placed my heart next to yours. Will you marry me?"

By this time, a crowd had formed around us. People were cheering and taking pictures. It was like a scene in a movie. "Yes, yes, of course I will marry you!" I blurted. He put the long-awaited ring on my left ring finger, jumped to his feet, and shouted in his booming voice, "She said yes, y'all!"

The crowd cheered, strangers hugged, and they congratulated us.

As I gazed at my engagement ring, I realized that my waiting time served a purpose. That time was necessary for my growth and maturation. It helped me focus on what was important in my life.

In a way, the best thing Gerald did in our journey was walk away and not return my phone calls when I rejected his first overture. It forced me to confront myself. If I had dated and married Gerald when we had first met, I would have sabotaged it for sure. I wasn't ready. Fear held my ability to truly love in bondage. Self-involvement clouded my judgment. I had to recognize these hard truths about myself. I had to open my heart to the power of God to bring deliverance.

I also realized that timing is part of God's purpose for us. Even a good seed will die if planted out of season. We have to submit to God's timing as well as His will for our lives. We can't get ahead of God or lag behind God. If we are not in sync with His timing, we could miss what He has for us.

On January 13, 2008, at the top of the Empire State Building, by God's grace, and His miraculous work of healing and restoration, I was finally ready. I was forty-two years old, and *finally* engaged to be married.

NINE

Overcoming

There is no question that your life will face both blessing and adversity. The question of whether you will succeed in life depends on how you overcome the tough times.

Adversity will come. It might be momentary, a temporary obstacle, or it might be a full stop, a roadblock of major proportions. It might be simply annoying, or it might be crushing. No matter what adversity you are facing right now, the key to your well-being and future success is how you overcome it.

If you are going through good times now, enjoy them. If you do so with the awareness that not all moments of your life will be so wonderful, it will make this season of blessing all the more precious.

If you are going through hard times now, understand these difficulties are what make you better, equip you for success down the road, and push you into a deeper relationship with God.

As I stood on a mountaintop of joy, I did not know I would all too soon experience the dry desert below.

The day after Gerald proposed, I booked the venue for our wedding. Because the beautiful venues in New York City book up quickly, I felt I had to move fast. I'd just been waiting on that all-important engagement ring. The next six months were a flurry of wedding planning, speaking, and my day-job responsibilities at CBS News. I couldn't get down the aisle fast enough. And my ovaries were aging by the minute.

Gerald and I talked extensively about having a family during our premarital counseling. We were very aware of our ages and the limitations that might place on our ability to conceive naturally. We wanted children but didn't know if those children would come to us by natural conception, medical intervention, or adoption. We agreed that we would try to conceive naturally for a year. If I didn't get pregnant, then we would begin to pray about Plan B or C. We agreed that after the wedding we would enthusiastically work on Plan A.

Who are you during adversity?

How can you become a better you by learning new ways of dealing with adversity?

By refocusing from "I won't make it" to "I will overcome," how might you remain hopeful through adverse circumstances?

In the meantime, we were learning how to blend our lives and "become one" as described in Genesis 2:24. It was no easy feat. We'd both been single for a long time. We had well-established routines. And we'd been the masters of our own domains for many years. Living with someone took a lot of adjustment for me. I had a roommate briefly in my twenties, but I'd lived alone for far longer. My stuff was exactly where I wanted it. Making room for Gerald in my home and life was more than a notion.

While our values and beliefs were, and are, nearly identical, our approach to life and living was, and is, vastly different. I am so grateful for the thorough premarital counseling that helped us avoid some conflicts and process others in a healthy, productive manner.

There was one conflict during our engagement that premarital counseling didn't address. I was in Connecticut at a women's conference hosted by my church. The Greater Allen A.M.E. Cathedral Women's Conference is a gathering of some of the most powerful women preachers in the country. Approximately a thousand women attend this annual weekend of worship, sermons, workshops, and fellowship. I was one of the workshop facilitators.

Before I tell you about the conflict, let me give you a little background.

I had sensed a call from God on my life in my teens. I didn't know exactly what He was calling me to do, but I believed I was supposed to minister the gospel of Jesus to people in some way. However, being a minister didn't appeal to me much then. I was afraid God was going to send me on the foreign mission field in some undeveloped African country where there was no electricity or pizza delivery.

I avoided answering this divine call for many years. Finally, in my early thirties, I disclosed to my pastor, Raphael Green, that I felt a call to ministry. At the time I lived in St. Louis and was attending Metro Christian Worship Center. I began the ministerial training class at Metro but put ministerial training on hold after I got the job at CBS and relocated to New York City.

After joining the Greater Allen A.M.E. Cathedral in Queens, New York, I disclosed to copastor Rev. Elaine Flake that I wanted to continue my ministerial training. Shortly after,

I entered the church's program and began working toward ordination.

I was still in the ministerial training process when Gerald and I got engaged. I loved being used by God to be a blessing to people. However, I sensed no call to pastor a church one day. I was content teaching and preaching and praying for people. That included teaching workshops at the Allen Women's Conference.

At the conference, I had spent a long day listening to dynamic female preachers, some of whom were also pastors. That night, while talking to Gerald on the phone, although I had no desire to be a pastor, I playfully asked a hypothetical question: "What would you say if God called me to pastor a church?" His response sucked all the fun out of the conversation.

"I don't see myself as a 'first husband,'" he deadpanned.

I was stunned. My flippant attempt at a fun chat suddenly turned serious.

"So, if I obeyed the call of God on my life, you would just walk away from this relationship . . . because I was being obedient to God?" I demanded.

Even though I had no plans or desire to pastor, I was incensed. What kind of person would break up with someone over doing what God called them to do? The rest of the conversation was very tense. I was offended. Gerald was resolute. The conversation ended abruptly. I didn't sleep for the rest of the night. I couldn't stop thinking, *Would I have to choose between ministry and marriage?* I was shaken.

The next morning, I went to brunch with the other conference speakers and workshop facilitators. As chatter happily flowed around me, I couldn't focus. The previous night's phone call with Gerald engulfed my thoughts. As I pushed eggs and grits around on my plate, I looked at the women seated at the table with me. It dawned on me that many were married.

*They surely would have advice on how to deal with my current
predicament,* I thought. So I told the women at the table about
the phone call and asked for their advice.

I will never forget what Bishop Cynthia James said. "Honey,
no man wants to sleep with his priest. He wants a wife, not
a pastor."

Her point was even if I did end up pastoring a church, my role
as a pastor would be completely different than my role as a wife.
Gerald was planning to marry a wife, not a pastor. She went on
to explain that I was foolish for having presented a hypothetical
situation to Gerald in the first place. If I had no intention of being
a pastor, why introduce a dilemma that doesn't exist?

The other women at the table offered their advice and perspectives as well. They admonished me to not take Gerald for
granted, to not try to control him or treat him like a girlfriend.
They cautioned me that, clearly, Gerald doesn't like hypotheticals. And apparently many other men don't either. Many
men are problem-solvers, they added. If it wasn't a real problem, then I shouldn't have broached it. One woman preacher
declared, "Process hypotheticals with your girlfriends." I am
grateful to the women in my life who taught me how to respond to Gerald. Their advice was greatly helpful. I felt better.
And I understood my mistake.

That night, when Gerald and I talked, I apologized for my
behavior. Apparently, God also had dealt with him. He was
not nearly as recalcitrant about the prospect of his future wife
being a pastor.

That was the first real test of our communication skills. There
would be many more. But we were equipped with communication
tools learned in premarital counseling that guided us through
disagreements without letting them become destructive and

vindictive. Even today, we really don't argue. Now, we disagree all the time. We can really annoy each other. But I am so grateful that we can express our emotions openly and constructively.

I like to say there is a third party in our marriage . . . the Holy Spirit. We are both careful to pray and consult the Holy Spirit for wisdom on how to fulfill our roles as husband and wife. Countless times I have asked God to help me understand Gerald when his behavior has confounded me. Every time, God reveals His truth to me and gives me direction in how to proceed.

We were reminded of the importance of God being a third party in marriage the day we got engaged. We were spending some time with a mentor and spiritual father of mine, Rev. Paul Leacock. Over brunch, Rev. Leacock shared his boundless wisdom about relationships and marriage. One of the illustrations he gave us was that we should look at ourselves as the two bottom corners of a triangle. God is at the apex, the top of the triangle. As we are intentional about getting closer to God, we naturally move closer to each other. I've never forgotten that advice, and make it a point to approach my role as a wife prayerfully.

With the guidance of other married women, and the Holy Spirit, I've learned that we must each take ownership of our issues in marriage and be willing to address them emotionally and spiritually—no matter what our mate is doing. Being in a covenant relationship means growing toward loving unconditionally. We have to be committed to do our part, regardless of what our partners are doing. At the very least, being committed to do the best we can to love unconditionally changes our perspective. Our focus shifts from "what's in this for me?" to "God, how do You want to demonstrate Your love in this relationship?"

Also, a mediator, like a counselor, pastor, or trusted friend is important to help couples navigate rough patches. Gerald and I are not in marriage counseling now, but we check in with the Greens (our premarital counselors) for tune-ups. And we seek advice when needed.

We have grown together in some wonderful ways. I feel like we are extensions of each other, even though we still maintain our unique individuality. But it has required careful intention to grow to this point. We've had to be willing to be transparent and vulnerable with each other. And we've had to be willing to compromise, admit wrong, back down, step up, and take constructive criticism and wise guidance.

I now clearly understand that in my twenties and thirties, I was looking for all the wrong things in a mate. Wealth, status, height, and eye color are all nice, but none of that makes a marriage last. It's important to find the person who will live in the mundane parts of life with you and not dip in and out of them or shun them altogether. I am blessed that my husband enjoys the small pleasures of life. He enjoys mowing the lawn, fixing a broken appliance, or washing the car. He loves that stuff. He finds pleasure in making a home and serving his family.

Gerald also calls me several times a day. He keeps me posted on his whereabouts and schedule changes. I don't require this of him. He wants me to feel secure in our relationship. He does this out of his love and devotion to me. These are the types of things that give a relationship longevity. Sadly, these are *not* the things most people have on their list when dating. I didn't. Yet thanks to God, I have a great husband for whom I am deeply grateful.

A few months before the wedding, my gynecologist recommended that I start trying to get pregnant immediately, even before marriage. I'd made an appointment with her to discuss contraception options once I got married. She knew conception was an uphill battle for someone of my age. So she prescribed a prenatal vitamin and admonished me: "Get to work. There's no guarantee that you can get pregnant at your age. The sooner you start trying the better your chances."

I began taking the vitamins, but I did *not* begin trying to get pregnant. Gerald and I both believed in waiting until marriage to have sex. We both had close calls and slipups in other relationships, but we were committed to living this Christian principle to the best of our abilities. Despite my gynecologist's suggestion, we committed to wait until our wedding night to start on baby-making. We trusted God. If it was His will for us to conceive, it would happen. After we got married.

We weren't even kissing on the lips during our engagement. Gerald had promised God that he wouldn't kiss a woman on the lips until he was at the altar marrying her. I know, this sounds bizarre! I completely agree. For me, part of the reason I could remain celibate all those years was the ability to kiss with abandon. Now I found myself engaged to someone who wouldn't kiss me on the lips. I was practically distraught.

To be fair, I knew about this pact Gerald had made with God because we'd been friends for fifteen years. I felt bad for his previous girlfriends. Now I was the un-kissed girlfriend. We pecked on the cheek, forehead, neck. Trust me. Not the same.

When we first started dating, I figured I could talk him out of what I felt was a ridiculous standard. We were planning to get married, after all! I tried to harass Gerald, seduce him (only for a kiss on the mouth), even shame him. Nothing worked. He was determined to keep his promise to God. Then it occurred to me: if any of my previous boyfriends with whom I had insisted we maintain celibacy had pressured me to have sex as much as I was pressuring Gerald to kiss me, I would have broken up with them because they did not respect my boundaries. So I gave up and accepted our no-kissing-on-the-lips status. I didn't agree with Gerald's standard, but I would respect it. Our first kiss was after we said, "I do." Kissing someone for the first time in front of nearly three hundred people is nerve-wracking. (Turns out, it was a great kiss!)

Gerald and I started enthusiastically trying to get pregnant on our wedding night. And pretty much every night (morning and afternoon) thereafter. My faith was strong. God had come through so many times throughout my life that I was convinced having a child would be no different. I began monitoring my ovulation closely. When the little ovulation stick displayed that an egg was likely ready, I demanded my husband perform "his duty" right away. I have to admit that this routine drained some of the fun out of it. As the months went by, and I kept getting my period, my faith wavered. Each time my period started, my heart broke a little more. I was on a daily roller coaster of optimistic lovemaking that turned to crushing disappointment of menstruation at month's end.

After ten months of obsessively trying to get pregnant, I finally threw in the towel. I still wanted a child, but I was beginning to think that conceiving naturally wasn't going to be how it happened. Of course, we'd been praying all those months to get pregnant. I would even silently pray during sex. *God, please, please, please let me get pregnant. Let there be one good egg in there.* After a while, I had to face the possibility that our family might come another way. We'd already discussed this possibility before we got married, but it was still disappointing.

Just as I had after all those failed tries to win the Miss Arkansas pageant, I submitted my will to God's will. I prayed, *"God, I give up. I want what you want for me. Your will be done."* I stopped monitoring my ovulation. I stopped demanding sex at just the right moment. I turned it over to the Lord. We didn't know if we would try fertility treatments or adoption. We began to pray for God's direction.

———

Then, in June 2009, I came home from work after a long, busy day. It had been stressful, so I decided I would go for a run to burn off some steam. As I changed into my running clothes, it occurred to me that my period was due but hadn't started. Nor did I feel the typical menstrual symptoms. *Could I maybe, possibly, perhaps, be pregnant?*

I didn't want to let myself believe it could be true. By this time, I'd taken so many pregnancy tests only to see one depressing pink line on the stick. I kept getting dressed to go on my run, but curiosity got the better of me. I had a pregnancy test left in the medicine cabinet. *What harm would it be to pee on the stick?* It was just sitting there. So I did. Then I waited the longest five minutes of my life. I left the stick in the bathroom and puttered around the apartment to pass the time. I tiptoed back into the bathroom when five minutes had elapsed. I stood at the door and stretched my neck to see the little window on the stick. I don't know why I didn't just walk up to the sink. I thought my eyes were fooling me. From the doorway, I thought I saw a second faint pink line.

I rushed to the sink, picked up the stick, closed my eyes, then opened them again. There it was . . . a second pink line. *Was I pregnant?* I let the stick sit for a few more minutes to see if the line would disappear. Nope. It was there to stay. But the second pink line was faint. I didn't dare get my hopes up yet. I called my cousin Monica, who had three children. I figured she was an expert in these things. I asked, "Monica, if there are two lines on a pregnancy test, even if the second line is faint, does that mean I could be pregnant? Are these things wrong?" "Nope," she replied. "Even if the line is faint, it's there. That means you're pregnant." We screamed and cried and praised God. Of course, I went to the drugstore and took another pregnancy test, just to be sure. Yep, I had a bun in the oven.

I was so excited and could not wait until Gerald came home from his business trip the next day. Since he was just a couple of hours away, I packed a picnic basket with sparkling cider, pastries, and the pregnancy test, and drove to him. I'd texted him, to make sure I could find him when I reached the destination. My excitement fueled my quest to see my husband ASAP. By the time I arrived, he'd wrapped up his meetings and we went back to his room. I told him that I missed him and, since he was so close, I wanted to see him.

Before I got on the road, I had cooked up a plan for telling him we were pregnant. I wrote this story about how I spent my day. At the bottom of the page was a cliffhanger. He would have to ask me for the next page when he read all the way down to find out how the story ends. I had taped the positive pregnancy test to a second page with "I'M PREGNANT!!!!" in big, bold letters.

Once we got to his hotel room, I made up a story about a writing assignment I was working on. I asked him if he would read the story and give me feedback. This was not unusual. Because I was a reporter at CBS, I wrote stories for a living. And I would often ask him to read something I was working on. My plan worked as I'd envisioned it. He read the first page. When he reached the bottom of the page, he flipped it over, looking for the end of the story. Noticing the blank backside, he looked up and asked about the remainder. I casually handed him the page that had our big news on it. It was folded in half. He unfolded it and saw the test stick and big letters. It took him a second to process what he was seeing. He looked up at me. "Really? Is this true?" I nodded. "Yes, Sweetheart, I'm pregnant."

He dropped the piece of paper, jumped up, and ran across the room, yelling, "Woooooo hooooo!" I sat alone on the side of the bed amused at his celebration. You'd have thought his favorite team just won the NBA championship. He finally came back to me. We hugged for a long time, crying, and thanking God.

For every mountaintop, there is a valley just below it. The hard truth is, life can sometimes feel cruel.

Life can be incredibly hard at times. Remembering how God brought us through past troubles can strengthen our faith, helping us trust Him despite our circumstances. God's past faithfulness is evidence of His future faithfulness. The Old Testament prophet declares,

> This I recall to my mind,
> Therefore I have hope.
>
> Through the LORD's mercies we are not consumed,
> Because His compassions fail not.
> They are new every morning;
> Great is Your faithfulness.
>   (Lamentations 3:21–23 NKJV)

We would do well to cherish and keepsake the good times God gives us. My advice to you is to store up a reservoir of memories of how God has been good and faithful to you. Remember and cherish these for the tough times, when they come.

Other than the customary "morning sickness" in those early weeks, my pregnancy went well. By God's grace, I had no complications. The baby girl growing inside me seemed to be healthy. Gerald and I were beyond excited and grateful. Our little family was finally growing. Lynlee Julia Bell was born at 12:42 p.m. on February 3, 2010. She came into this world making a lot of noise, and hasn't stopped since.

As so many parents know, an addition of a child to our home changed everything, in some wonderful and some exhausting ways. After an eleven-week maternity leave, I went back to work at CBS. And Gerald and I went back to work trying to have another child. Since Lynlee came into our lives, we dared to believe that we could get pregnant again. At forty-four, I gave birth to a normal, healthy baby with no fertility assistance. If God did it once, He could do it again, we believed.

I discovered I was pregnant for a second time just before Lynlee's first birthday. We were elated. I was forty-five years old, but all hesitations about my age as it related to my fertility had disappeared. We had a vibrant, delightful toddler as proof that miracles do happen. So I wasted no time telling family and close friends I was pregnant with our second child. I had every reason to believe that we would have another great outcome.

———

Eleven days after Lynlee's first birthday, I began to bleed. I rushed to see my ob-gyn. To our horror, I was miscarrying. The process had already started, and nothing could be done to stop it. It was Valentine's Day. I took the day off from work. There was no way I could ignore the tragedy happening in my body and pretend everything was OK. But I didn't want to lay around at home either. So Gerald and I spent the afternoon driving around neighborhoods looking at houses for sale. We'd already started house hunting in anticipation of our growing family. We strolled through a few open houses as if all was well. Nothing could have been further from the truth.

We were devastated.

I was shocked because my faith had been so strong. Just like with my mom's cancer, I was absolutely convinced God was going to work another miracle. When it didn't work out. I was floored. The miscarriage happened fairly early in the pregnancy. We hadn't even heard the baby's heartbeat. My ob-gyn consoled me, "Well, you've carried to term once, there's a chance you can do it again. There's no harm in trying again." But my heart was tender. I didn't want another disappointment. Gerald and I agreed that we would just not think about it for a while.

Life went on. We were happily distracted by the wonder of watching our beautiful little girl grow. Over time, the sting of the loss of the second baby faded. Then in 2012, I got pregnant again. We were cautiously excited. I tried to do everything I could to protect the life growing in me: I slowed my schedule; I ate as healthfully as possible; and I tried to get more sleep, or at least as much as is possible while parenting a two-year-old.

This time, we only told a few very close friends and family, mainly those we thought would pray for us and the baby. I breathed a little easier with each passing week, as I progressed through the tricky first trimester. It was during this time that I got the job as an anchor for Arise News. I hadn't even told my new boss I was pregnant. I was waiting for the second trimester to arrive, to be more certain the baby would survive.

October 2012 arrived, and I was at the end of my first trimester. I'd planned on telling my new boss I was pregnant the next day. I thought I could finally breathe a sigh of relief. *We are out of the woods*, I thought. But the unthinkable happened. I began to bleed a little. My obstetrician saw me right away. She squirted warm jelly on my belly, which was just starting to poke out a little. She ran the ultrasound probe back and forth over my lower abdomen. I held my breath. My doctor's facial expression was neutral. If something was wrong, it wasn't evident on her face. She kept checking and checking again. She pushed several buttons, retaking measurements. I knew she wouldn't speak until she was ready.

Finally, she put away the probe, wiped off the jelly, and told me I could sit up. She told me my baby was still there and had a detectable heartbeat. But . . . it was faint. And the baby was not the size she would expect at this point in the pregnancy. She added, "I'm so sorry, Debbye, your baby is not going to survive. It's dying."

No, no, no!

I couldn't believe this was happening again. My doctor offered to perform a procedure to speed the process. I declined the offer. If there was still a heartbeat, then as far as I was concerned, there was still hope. I told my doctor I would wait and see what happened. She informed me that it may be a few days or perhaps a week, but I was going to miscarry. I didn't want to believe that. My faith didn't have room for such news.

I went home and told Gerald what the doctor said. We shut ourselves up in our bedroom and cried out to God. We prayed for our little struggling baby. We begged God to perform a miracle, to reverse the process that had started. I had seen God heal my rash, my sister's health, and countless others' illnesses. I knew He was capable of performing a miracle. I implored God to please let me have this baby. I just couldn't bear the thought of a second miscarriage. I don't know how long we prayed, but day had turned to night. Our babysitter had been watching Lynlee while we sought God. We finally said amen, wiped our tears, and went out to the living room to play with the little girl we had.

Ten days later, the miscarriage began. It was October 27, 2012, just as the front edge of Superstorm Sandy came roaring into New Jersey and New York. Because I was so far along in the pregnancy, the process was much harder. I began having contractions as though I was giving birth. I guess I was giving birth, just way too early. After several hours of hard labor, we finally decided I should go to the hospital. We drove through barren streets as the howling winds of Sandy were whipping through trees and tossing around debris. Government officials had repeatedly warned citizens to stay at home and off the roads. We had no choice but to venture out.

We arrived safely to the Hackensack University Hospital. Gerald stayed in the waiting room to entertain Lynlee while I was taken back to a treatment area for an examination. An ER doctor gave me something for my discomfort. After an ultrasound, I was told that the baby was gone. Now, I just had to wait for my body to finish the sad process. I was crestfallen. The first miscarriage was hard. This one was a punch in the gut.

There are painful tragedies and experiences that seem like no words will ever soothe; despair so deep that there is no visible way of escape. But there is hope. There is help.

What helped me? I trusted God. I didn't understand why I lost those babies. But I trusted God.

The grief this time was similar to the pain of my mom's death. It was all-consuming, unexpected, even a little cruel. But this grief was also different. I had a reservoir of experience from Mommy's death, which made the grieving easier this time. I had history with God in dealing with loss that somehow helped me walk this path.

I opened my heart to His healing love. I poured out my sorrow, knowing He is near the brokenhearted (Psalm 34:18).

During an intense time of affliction, Job declared, "Though He slay me, yet will I trust Him" (Job 13:15 NKJV). I'd come to better understand that Scripture while mourning the loss of our precious babies. And I'd had enough previous experience with God to know that even in gut-wrenching loss, He is still faithful. In Isaiah God assures, "When you pass through the waters, I will be with you." (Isaiah 43:2 NKJV).

And He was.

I knew I would be whole again.

Someday.

TEN

Perseverance

The road to success is paved with perseverance. Choose a stick-to-it, never-quit attitude to reach your dream destination. Too often we wish for, and even pray for, an easy life without challenges or hardships. While that sounds great, in most cases, it's simply unrealistic.

The very definition of perseverance includes opposition.

I learned this lesson in spades as I trained for and ran six marathons.

Running a marathon is daunting, overwhelming. The race becomes its own story of perseverance—overcoming fatigue, body aches, and fear—one mile at a time.

I ran the New York City Marathon for the second time in 2005. It was my fourth marathon in twelve months.

For many years, I had wanted to train for and run a marathon. It is one of those aspirations born of my competitive nature and goal-oriented personality. I am always looking for the next challenge; something to expand my borders. I have great respect for athletes of any kind. And long-distance runners, especially, have held a certain mystique for me. I watch the marathon competition at each Summer Olympics and cry when the runners cross the finish line. I can almost feel their sense of accomplishment, relief, and joy. What a great sacrifice to train to run twenty-six miles.

Since I lived in the New York City area, I decided to enter the 2004 New York City Marathon. I wanted to know what it felt like to actually cross that finish line for myself! Entrants are chosen lottery-style because so many people from around the globe register to race. About one-hundred thousand people apply to run. That year, around forty thousand would be chosen. I threw my hat in the ring.

At this point in my life, my workout schedule was spotty at best. I was running on the treadmill for thirty minutes at most, two or three times a month. That was less than once a week! Over the years, I'd gained a lot of weight. I love to eat! The richer, fattier, and sweeter the food the better! I had very little to no discipline about my eating habits and no real fitness regimen. That was a recipe for disaster—and a surefire way to never reach my marathon goals. Since becoming Miss America, I had grown from a petite size to a plus size. As I approached the big four-oh in 2005, I knew I needed to address some bad habits and get control of my health.

I started running three times a week. My earliest runs were just less than three miles long. I thought I was going to die! But slowly my body adjusted to the increased activity. And within a month, I was actually enjoying my runs.

All of the principles of life and success I've shared in this book come together in the challenge of running a marathon. It's a good description of the challenge and success that we encounter.

Just preparing to run is part of the story. It says, "I'm not satisfied with where I am." I have failed but I have faith I can do better and I am determined to do something different with my life. It also demands patience, as your training brings you to plateaus and roadblocks along the way.

Actually *entering* a marathon takes courage.

———

After two and a half months of progressive training, I received word that I made the cut. I was a bona fide entrant into the New York City Marathon. I was so excited, I went running through the halls of CBS screaming, jumping, and laughing. Then it hit me, *I am rejoicing because I now have to run twenty-six miles.* By then, my training was getting serious. I ran two five-mile runs during the week and a long run on the weekends. I was running from ten to fourteen miles at a time on those longer runs. I loved it. I used the time to pray, praise, sing, and think. Some of the best devotional time I've ever had was on the streets of New York City, running.

Finally, race day arrived, November 7, 2004. From beginning to end, running the New York City Marathon was a thrilling experience! With thirty-six thousand runners, it takes a while for everyone to even get across the starting line. I began my real, timed marathon about ten minutes after the starting gun went off. I can't fully express how exciting this was. The views of the city were spectacular. And the spectators along the way were extraordinary. Two million spectators. All cheering and yelling words of encouragement.

> Who are the people running alongside you as you dream big and pursue success?
>
> How could a change of pace help you better persevere?
>
> By refocusing from "sprint" to "marathon," how might you gain a new appreciation for long-term goals?

But at mile nineteen, slowly my legs began to cramp. My *whole* leg; my quads, calves, inner thighs . . . *everything*. It eventually got so bad that I could barely stand. I didn't know how I was going to keep going, but I knew I was not going to quit. I stretched a bit and continued . . . at a hobble. I walked a mile (to give my legs a rest) then tried to run again. This cycle of walking, trying to run, then cramping like you wouldn't believe kept up for the next five miles. I walked most of it. But by mile twenty-four and a half, I was bound and determined to run across the finish line. I'd worked too hard to give up now.

I started running. I cannot describe the pain. But I wouldn't stop. I was running, crying, praying, begging God, and saying over and over, "I can do all things! I can do all things!" When the pain became excruciatingly unbearable, I walked a few feet then kept running. With a little less than a mile to go, I gritted my teeth, started running, and gutted it out. I ran across that finish line. The feeling was pure exhilaration. No sooner had I crossed the finish line than my calf cramps returned. Two medics had to catch me before I fell.

I don't know why I had the cramps. It is truly a mystery to me. I had diligently trained for seven months. Along the way, I ran eighteen, twenty, twenty-one, and twenty-three miles. Some of those distances more than once! I never cramped while training. Not even once. That is how life is sometimes. We prepare, practice, and train, and still life throws us a curveball. The ball is not the issue. It's how we handle it. I had never experienced cramping before, but I refused to let the cramps get the best of me. Don't let "cramps" get the best of you either.

Even if you have to walk part of the way, keep going.

I ran two more marathons in short order afterward: the Los Angeles Marathon in March 2005, and the Steamtown Marathon in Scranton, Pennsylvania, in October 2005. Every marathon has taught me a new lesson about life. My very first marathon had taught me I could set what seemed like an impossible goal, achieving it through hard work and sheer determination. My second marathon taught me I could learn from previous mistakes, improve, run a smarter race, and get a better result. My third marathon taught me that overconfidence and inexperience can lead to a result that's slightly inferior to my high expectations.

For that third race, I figured that since I had already run two marathons, my finish time was bound to only get better. I had run my second marathon forty minutes faster than the first one. I had hoped to run the third marathon at least that much faster than the second. But that didn't happen. Why? I underestimated the drain of running downhill for eight straight miles. The marathon in Scranton, Pennsylvania, is largely a downhill run. Figuring that running downhill is a lot easier than running a flat or hilly course, I thought I would surely have the personal best time of my life. Wrong.

Running downhill is hard on the thighs. Trust me when I tell you this. My thighs began to burn at around mile thirteen, and they hurt like they were on fire for the rest of the marathon. Having a searing burn shoot through my quadriceps muscles with every impact for more than thirteen miles was not fun. But I finished the run, just not in record time. In fact, my time was twelve minutes slower than the Los Angeles time. And the Los Angeles course is a flat course. Who knew running a flat course would be easier than running downhill?

My fourth marathon, the 2005 NYC Marathon, taught me that more than personal goals, more than individual competitiveness, more than overconfidence, going the distance on the value of my word and loyalty to friendship conquers all. This is where I learned significance is more important than success.

After my first marathon, a precious friend of mine, Brenda Green, was so inspired by my weight loss that she vowed to run the NYC Marathon the next year. I told her in a show of support that, if she followed through, I would run the marathon with her. And I promised that I would stay with her the whole way. Soon, I learned that Brenda's running pace was much slower than mine. Because of my less-than-stellar finish time in the Steamtown Marathon, I really wanted to run a good race at the 2005 NYC Marathon. But that would mean leaving my friend behind, so I could have a better time to brag about. I began to fret over asking Brenda if she would mind if I ran on my own, so I could improve my time. I would be going back on my word. I felt caught in a dilemma. I talked to friends about it. I prayed about it.

Brenda had been steadfastly training, gaining confidence and excitement. The closer we got to the race, the more excited—and anxious—she became. I never had the courage to ask her my big question. Finally, I decided I would broach the subject on the day before the marathon. Another friend was running with us, too, so she wouldn't really be left alone. I would simply present my case, ask her permission, and accept her answer, no matter what it would be. I never got the chance to ask my question. When I picked her up on the morning before the race, the first thing she said to me was, "Debbye, I am a little nervous. But I know I can make it with you and Kelly with me." That settled it. I couldn't possibly get out of this. She needed me more than I needed a better time. This was a hard pill to swallow, I must admit.

On the day of the race, we were all excited. At first, it still bothered me that I couldn't run full out. But after a few miles, I realized that this time, the marathon was not about me. So I relinquished my selfish ambitions and grandiose ideas and decided to just be there for my friend. We laughed. We talked. And we ran that marathon, one mile at a time. Brenda was doing pretty well but her pace was very slow. At mile twenty, her resolve began to waver.

"I'm out of gas, Debbye," she said.

"You can make it!" I tried encouraging her.

By mile twenty-two, I could see she was really starting to struggle. So I told her that we were going to finish, no matter what. I sang to her. I quoted Scripture. And we kept running. Finally, we made the last turn before heading to the finish line. By this time, most spectators had gone home. There were just a handful of people watching the last of us as we approached the end of the race. Just before the finish line, we grabbed hands. We'd started this journey together and we were going to finish together. And we did, hand in hand. There were shouts of victory, tears of relief, and exhausted muscles. But we made it . . . together.

Success is not always what we think it is.

That day I learned that sometimes true victory is measured by how and with whom you finish the race, not by the speed with which you finish it. Being supportive that day was more important than being impressive. And putting another's success before my own took more self-discipline and perseverance than increasing my speed. I will forever cherish this marathon. It was a success. It was also significant because the success was about more than me and my accomplishment.

I ran two more marathons over the next two years—a total of six. Alas, my knees revolted. I started experiencing extreme knee pain and had to give up long-distance running. To this day, I miss those long runs. Of course, over time, I gained back the weight I lost while running, and then some. So I decided to enter a half marathon in 2018. This time, I planned to walk, not run. I wanted a challenge and some much-needed exercise. I put myself on a training schedule and looked forward to the big day.

There were many other walkers, so I felt completely comfortable walking instead of running. I started the race with a group of women who had trained together. They seemed to know each other well. They were very friendly and welcoming, asking me about my life and family. I enjoyed the conversation, but those ladies were not walking as fast as I wanted to walk. I'd trained at a certain pace and wanted to finish in a certain time. After a mile or two, I quietly quickened my pace and pulled ahead of them. As I began to make up some ground, I could see another group of walkers in front of me. I was gaining ground, but their pace was a little faster than mine. I held steady at the pace that was comfortable to *me*. This meant that I walked the half marathon alone.

I started to wonder if I should change my pace so that I could be with a group of people. Many thoughts bombarded me as I walked. This sounds like a small thing now, but at the time I was wracked with conflict over whether to slow down or speed up. Finally, I prayed and asked God, "Lord, what should I do?" Immediately I heard in my heart, "Run your own race." This was my race. That freed me. It removed the pressure to somehow match someone else's pace. I knew the pace that was right for me. I resolved that I would walk at the pace that I'd trained and stop worrying about who was behind me or ahead of me. I determined that I was going to "run" my own race, even if it meant I walked the half marathon alone.

This should be true for our lives too. We might have friends who are not as motivated as we are, and it's tempting to slow down in order to not stand out. Or we see people achieving more than we seem to be able to achieve, so we look for ways to keep up and match their accomplishments. Either scenario can lead to frustration. The real goal in life should be to run the race that we were each put on this earth to run. Don't worry about who is ahead of you or behind you. You do your race. I will do mine. Together, we will persevere at a God-honoring pace.

That is the essence of excellence. I've learned that excellence is often lonely. No one else can travel the path that God has chosen for each individual. There won't always be someone to put in the extra hours, the hard work, the greater sacrifice with us. We have to have the courage to go by ourselves, if that's what it takes. Yes, it can get lonely, but we are not alone. God will never leave nor forsake us. His Spirit will be our comfort and guide. And God sends the people we need just at the time that we need them. So run your race of life at your pace—and persevere through each milestone.

I mentioned finish times when I ran marathons or walked the half marathon. Time is a factor in any race. But don't worry if you feel like you've lost time in your life. Nothing in my life has come quickly or easily—I have to always remind myself of that fact.

It took seven years to win Miss America. It took fifteen years to realize the man of my dreams was already in my life. It took more than a decade to finally anchor the news. And I am still waiting for some other goals and accomplishments. Perseverance in significance requires time, sometimes lots of it.

But, passage of time is nothing to God. He is a redeemer of time. It's never too late. As long as there is still breath in your lungs and your heart is beating, then God can redeem the time for you. Even when we think it's too late, it is not too late. God created time. And God controls time. He can supernaturally restore lost time. So take heart. If you are still alive, then there's still time to live in the purpose for which God created you. Being alive is evidence that you still have purpose. God is faithful to complete the good work that He has begun in you (Philippians 1:6).

Success from a biblical perspective is not simply the accumulation of things or the achievement of power and status, nor is it defined by our education, careers, jobs, homes, or stock portfolios. Divine success is being who and what God created us to be.

Meanwhile, true greatness is service to our fellow humans—being kind to one another, extending ourselves to people. Greatness is living our lives for something bigger than just ourselves, our appetites and desires.

Our ultimate success is to fulfill God's purpose to our generation. In other words, to do what we were put on earth to do. Fame, wealth, education, power are all great. I am not knocking any of those. But they are not reliable indicators of living a truly successful life. There are a lot of famous or wealthy or powerful people who are lonely, miserable, and lost.

When I finally see the Lord face-to-face after I leave this earth, I will have many questions for Him. Why did my mother die at age fifty-five? Why did I raise one child, instead of three? Why was I single for so long? Why can't vegetables taste as good as pie and doughnuts? Chances are you'll have questions of your own because life can present some perplexing and disappointing circumstances.

I have questions. But I do not question the goodness of my heavenly Father. I do not question His love and power. He has demonstrated His faithfulness more times than I can count, more than this book could hold. I pray that I have a long life ahead of me, but if my life on earth ended today, I can declare with confidence that God's goodness is unwavering. I have a much greater understanding of what David must have been feeling when he wrote, "I have been young, and now am old;

yet I have not seen the righteous forsaken, nor his descendants begging bread. He is ever merciful, and lends; and his descendants are blessed" (Psalm 37:25–26 NKJV).

It's a truth I learned growing up in Gussie Turner's household. I am who I am today because of her prayers. Her faith and real-life example of Christ inspired my perseverance as both a child and an adult. I thank God for placing me under her tutelage. More so, I am grateful to our good God who has never left or forsaken me since the day I sat at my kitchen table and became a Christian at age seven.

Back then, I did not know my life's purpose. I had no clue I'd be on the Miss America stage accepting the crown. I had no idea how God would use my platform to position me to live a life of perseverance even as He graciously allows me to inspire other believers to know and trust Him. Winning Miss America was a highlight of my life, but only one of the faith milestones I achieved.

One thing I have discovered: the crown of victory *never* goes to the person who quits before or during a race. The crown belongs to the victor—and we are victors in Christ. We win by His rules, His way. There are a lot of things in this world and in my life's experience that I don't understand, nor can I explain. But I know for sure that God is good. All the time. I stake my life on this truth.

Acknowledgments

The very fact that you are reading this proclaims the multitude of family members, friends, encouragers, scolders, editors, marketers, artists, and leaders who carefully shepherded me through the daunting, arduous, and liberating process of writing this book.

To echo the words of churchgoers of old in the Pentecostal tradition, "First, I give honor to God, my Creator, Redeemer, and everlasting Father." I simply would not be here if it weren't for the grace, goodness, and faithfulness of God, through His Son Christ Jesus. To God be all the glory!

Thank you to Matthew Parker for sharing my proposal with the Voices publishing board. And a big hug and debt of gratitude to Khary Bridgewater, who listened to me go on and on about my life while we were both waiting on our daughters to finish their piano lessons. Like many others, he declared to me that I should write a book. When I told him that I'd tried for years to find a publisher, he introduced me to Joyce Dinkins.

Joyce is the Our Daily Bread Ministries Voices Collection Executive Editor. She was my editor on this project, and now my dear sister in Christ. To know Joyce is to love her. Her gentle, steady way of encouraging, prodding, and challenging me was a comfort and an inspiration. Thank you, Joyce, for first acknowledging God in all you do. Thank you for believing in me and the book you knew was in me. Thank you for listening to and *hearing* me. This process was a joy, in large part, because of your guidance.

A found a new sister in the writing process. Lisa Crayton, my developmental coeditor, helped me find my voice. Her insightful and discerning questions during our many conversations pulled out of me a deeper story than I would have accessed on my own. Thank you, Lisa, for operating in your tremendous divine gift and anointing.

Thank you to the wonderful team at Our Daily Bread Ministries that surrounded this project, paid relentless attention to every detail, and poured your heart and excellence into it. The accuracy, beauty, and creativity of this book are due in large part to the eagle eyes and talent of Dawn Anderson, Heather Brewer, and Patti Brinks. A hearty thanks to John van der Veen, and Bobby Palosaari. Thank you to former Our Daily Bread Ministries publisher, Ken Petersen, for believing my story was worth telling and for being committed enough to make the necessary changes to my manuscript to set my book up for success.

I am indebted to the current publisher, Chriscynethia Floyd. Thank you, Chriscynethia, for making time to get to know me and hear my heart. You had courageous faith in me. I am humbled and profoundly grateful.

Thanks to my agent on this project, Tom Winters. Thank you, Tom, for taking my frantic, out-of-the-blue call and agreeing to represent me.

Thank you to my sister-friends, Jeanne, Nichole, Aldrena, Candace, Deborah, and Suzette (my actual sister), who encouraged me, pushed me, and prayed this book out into the world.

Shout out and much love to photographer extraordinaire, Suzy Gorman, and the glam squad, Everett Johnson, Khadijah Amirah, and Chrissie Beard Wojciechowski, who made sure I was "tight and right" for the cover photo shoot.

And finally, special thanks and eternal appreciation goes to my beautiful daughter, Lynlee, who is a daily inspiration, and to my adoring and adorable husband, Gerald. Thank you for listening to me read chapter after chapter as I was writing the manuscript. Thank you for giving me the time and space to write without complaining about fast-food dinners. Thank you for the countless prayers and support through this long process.

The danger in naming names as I express my thanks is leaving someone out. So, to everyone who provided a listening ear, encouraging word, or broad shoulders upon which I stand, I thank you from the depths of my soul.

And I would like to thank the countless people who over the years, after hearing me share my story, encouraged and challenged me by saying, "You should write a book." It only took thirty years. But here it is.

To invite Debbye to speak at your next event
or to follow her on social media, visit

www.debbyeturnerbell.com

LinkedIn: Debbye Turner Bell

Instagram: @DebbyeTurnerBell

Facebook: @DebbyeTB

Twitter: @DrDebbye